Disasters at Sea

Dag Pike

Published by Adlard Coles Nautical
an imprint of A & C Black Publishers Ltd
38 Soho Square, London W1D 3HB
www.adlardcoles.com

Copyright © 2008 Dag Pike

First edition 2008

ISBN 978-0-7136-8878-8

The right of the author to be identified as the author
of this work has been asserted by him in accordance with
the Copyright, Designs and Patents Act, 1988.

A CIP catalogue record for this book is available from
the British Library.

This book is produced using paper that is made from
wood grown in managed, sustainable forests. It is natural,
renewable and recyclable. The logging and manufacturing
processes conform to the environmental regulations of
the country of origin.

Design and Concept by Fred Barter ARCA at Bosun Press.

Typeset in 10pt Minion.
Printed and bound by South China Printing Co Ltd. China

Adlard Coles Nautical
London

Disasters at Sea

Dag Pike

Including reports from MAIB
(the Marine Accident
Investigation Branch)

CONTENTS

Rescues

Storms

Survival

Collision

The Future

Index

Introduction

Disaster is a constant threat when you go to sea. Most of the time everything works and a voyage goes smoothly. But dangers are all around, and the consequences of getting it wrong can be very serious. The uncaring line between survival and calamity can often be very fine. Even modern technology holds no guarantee of security, and most sailors have tales to tell of misfortune or near-tragedy during their time at sea.

When man first started exploring the oceans, there was every opportunity for disaster. Craft were solely at the mercy of the wind. Charts were rudimentary or non-existent – the mere thought of making a landfall without them is completely beyond modern navigators. Being at sea without a weather forecast, or relying on your own weather skills, is also alien to today's sailor. But those pioneering seafarers made it work, or at least the ones who survived did – and it is only the successful ones we tend to hear about. There were countless poor souls that never made it, lost in circumstances never recorded.

Electronic wizardry

Today we go to sea with the latest technology at our fingertips. We have reasonably accurate weather forecasts for up to five days ahead. The charts we use are accurate and up-to-date. We carry electronic wizardry that plots our course and detects other vessels seemingly miraculously.

Yet still disaster strikes with uncomfortable regularity. You only have to look at the casualty pages of *Lloyds List,* the shipping newspaper, to realise that major incidents occur on an almost daily basis. These are so many, they often fill a whole page – and those are only the entries for commercial shipping. Fishing vessels are equally vulnerable. Yachts too have their fair share of mishaps. So if our modern world is so risk-averse, how are such casualties tolerated and why do they happen?

In theory, there is no technical reason why disasters should occur. Modern ships and small craft are well built. They have enough position information to locate themselves anywhere in the world to within a few metres. They have very clever radar to help avoid other vessels. They have communications systems for keeping up to date with the latest weather and navigation information. On the face of it, there is no excuse for getting it wrong.

Undoubtedly, the weakest link in all of this technology is the human element. Just as human ingenuity coordinates all the different workings of a vessel and makes the decisions, so human frailty finds fallibilities, defeating technology at a stroke.

Human error

It is reckoned that up to 80% of all casualties are caused by human error. From personal experience, I would actually put that closer to 100%. The 80% relates to cases with direct evidence of human cause – not recognising a collision risk until it is too late, or failing to heed deteriorating weather conditions. Navigation mistakes also fall into this category. So do the not so obvious 'accidents' of engine failure or hull breakage. Somewhere the designer got his figures wrong, or the maintenance person did not do his job properly. All of which means that whoever was assessing the risks made a wrong call and misjudged them. In my eyes these are all human error. And in nearly every case, a disaster at sea can be traced directly or indirectly to human failings of one sort or another.

Both shipping and yachting are unique in the relaxed way that they are regulated. By comparison, all other forms of transport have pretty strict control. Aircraft, for instance, are guided along routes that are dictated from the ground. Collision avoidance is not up to pilots, but handled by ground control – and most of the time, it works. Trains are kept on the straight and narrow by the rails and a signalling system. Even road traffic is strictly controlled when compared to shipping.

Ships and yachts, on the other hand, are pretty much free to roam the oceans as they please. The only significant form of control is in the Vessel Separation Systems that are used in narrow seaways and some harbour approaches. Even with these, it is the ship's navigator who determines the point and method of entry, the course to be followed and the collision avoidance tactics. The actual level of control is minimal and all safety measures depend totally on the navigator. It is hardly surprising, then, that some navigators on either ships or boats find they cannot cope, nudging misfortune nearer. Add in substandard ships, poorly equipped yachts, people with little or no qualification or ability, and you have a recipe for disaster.

Testing ships

On the design and construction side of the industry, I find it quite incredible that nearly every ship is built as a one-off. There have been some attempts over the years to build ships to standard designs, but even these make little or no attempt at prototype testing. The yacht and powerboat industry is closer to standardisation because each popular design is eventually built in big numbers. Though even then, the principle of developing a prototype first and putting it through a series of exhaustive trials and tests at sea is not even considered.

The only time a ship or a small craft is tested in rough seas is when the owner or the skipper runs it into bad weather. Compare this to the automobile and aircraft industries, where prototype testing takes months and a new design is subjected to near-destruction testing to eliminate problems before entering service.

Alongside such levels of integrity, marine development is in the dark ages. True, the classification societies do their bit by establishing standards that help eliminate failure in construction. But none of these covers the same vessels in their behaviour at sea. Rough sea experience can certainly show what works and what doesn't in terms of hull design. Even so, I have come across some very questionable designs during my experience of powerboat testing.

Lifeboats that go out to rescue others in the worst possible conditions are one of the few exceptions to this pattern, and their prototypes are thoroughly tested in the worst conditions. When working for the RNLI I had a simple brief when evaluating new designs: 'Go out in the worst conditions you can find, and see what happens.'

You can imagine the hazards that lack of standardisation throws up. Picture a ship that leaves Rotterdam with a new crew, entirely green to her. With luck they might have 24 hours to become familiar with her; quite a challenge with no standardisation in bridge equipment or its layout, or even in the control systems, radar, or the electronic charts carried.

The crew are on their own

The pilot might take the ship out to sea successfully, but after that the crew are on their own. They are now in at the deep end, in some of the busiest waters in the world. It could be dark too, an added trial when using new equipment and learning how it works, at the same time as navigating safely through ships coming at them from all directions. Is it any wonder that accidents happen as often as they do?

Believe it or not, yacht and fishing boat skippers have the advantage here. They tend to use the same vessel and equipment whenever they go to sea, so they are more likely to be familiar with it. Yachtsmen, though, may have a considerable gap between periods at sea, so they may have to go through the learning process again.

You have to wonder whether accidents resulting from this kind of scenario should really be classed as 'human error'. On the face of it, the crew might be negligent or incompetent. But is it fair to blame the operator who has to use equipment in this way? The operator (and in most cases that means the captain or the skipper, because that is where the buck stops) has to make the best of the circumstances he is presented with.

It would be a brave captain who refused to go to sea because his crew had not had time to familiarise themselves with the equipment. In addition to an unfamiliar ship, there is also the possibility that the officers on the bridge may already have been on duty for long periods before the vessel sailed. Fatigue is a recognised major cause of accidents at sea, not easy to deal with when time is money and business is highly competitive.

Fatigue is a major problem on fishing boats as well. And, just as easily, a problem on yachts. In both cases, fatigue is most likely on the return from a long voyage, during the critical stage of entering harbour. It is not surprising that so many disasters occur in these last moments of a voyage – as I have seen myself in the days before radar, coming up the English Channel in fog. In these conditions, the pressure on the crew is very high and continuous, and so stressful that mistakes are easily made. The number of cases in which craft, particularly fishing vessels, pass the wrong side of channel piers on entering harbour is testament to this problem.

On fishing boats and yachts, the pressure comes from just wanting to get into harbour and stop. For full-size ships, there is the added pressure of keeping to tight schedules. The costs of running a ship are so huge that a few hours' delay can cost a fortune, especially should missing a tide extend the hold-up. On passenger ships, any delays that set the schedules back have even bigger consequences – missed connections, cancelled meetings, lost business – so the pressure is really on. Although this is a relatively new demand in shipping services, the challenge to tired crews is even greater.

Casualty figures

When you look at the statistics, the picture gets even more serious. Figures from the International Maritime Organisation (IMO), an international body set up by the United Nations to oversee safety at sea, suggest that over a five year period there were 1,500 accidents at sea that could be classed as serious. That equates to 300 per year, or almost one every day.

Worse, these accidents happen to ships that are supposedly manned by professional crews with the latest equipment after passing rigorous safety inspections. Even more incredible is that these casualty numbers appear to be acceptable, with very little being done to reduce them. I can accept that finding international agreement for improvements is difficult, but the changes in safety seem more focused on detail than in solving overall problems.

The British Nautical Institute has carried out a study into the effect of over-reliance on electronic navigation and they quote casualty figures from the International Union of Marine Insurers. According to these, total losses through grounding and collisions rose at the rate of 4–5% over a four year period. Cases involving serious damage are also rising, but at a slightly lower rate. The Nautical Institute says, 'A startling statistic noted in the investigation is the large number of collisions that occurred when the officer of the watch was unaware of the other vessel until the time of the collision.'

Poor watchkeeping

Though that seems hard to believe, it also suggests that standards of lookout have deteriorated sharply. Almost half of all collisions were caused through poor watchkeeping, according to the British Marine Accident Investigation Branch, citing cases where the watchkeeper was asleep, fatigued, absent, distracted or totally disengaged – you have to wonder what that last phrase means!

But I do not find it difficult to imagine situations like this occurring on either ships or leisure craft. I have vivid recollections of coming back from the Cod War off Iceland on a ship where the bridge was deserted at 11.00 in the morning and a party was in full swing down below! Pity the poor yacht or small craft unlucky enough to be in the path of such a ship.

Going to sea is a tough enough life, and there is clearly a need to relax from the strict routines necessary to keep ships and yachts safe. I have little doubt in my mind, though, that many accidents are caused by the now 'acceptable' situation where there is only one person on watch at any time. When corners get cut, mistakes are made. And the assumption that modern electronic systems can do the work of a watchkeeper is misplaced. If anything, the workload is increased, not reduced, removing most of the excuses that might be made should things go wrong.

So over the years, the pressure on captains and skippers has changed. In the old days it was just getting the navigation right, finding harbour, and using your best skills and knowledge to complete the voyage. Mistakes were a sort of acceptable risk back then, when it took your best judgement to complete a voyage successfully.

Mistakes are less acceptable

With the advent of modern electronic systems, mistakes are much less acceptable and the pressure to perform is intense. Delays because of weather are not tolerated in the same way, so the crews push the envelope of performance to limits that were previously not acceptable. Which raises the question: what are acceptable risks for the operation of ships and small craft? And where do the limits of such risk lie?

With aviation, the long programme of testing and evaluation has determined precisely what an aircraft can and cannot do. In the marine world, there is no such assessment, no measure of where the limits of performance may lie. For example, there is no assessment of how hard you can push a ship in bad weather before it breaks. That judgement is left entirely to the experience of the captain.

Similarly in smaller craft, it is the physical pain and discomfort tolerances of the crew that usually indicate where the limits are – providing a degree of security in performance, because the crew usually give up before the vessel does! However, when the crew get to that stage, their focus is more on outlasting the unpleasantness than in longer-term problem solving.

This book does not try to offer solutions to these problems, though I like to feel that by raising them – and showing examples of how and why things go wrong at sea – it will at least generate a more acute awareness of the problems and risks. Ever since the *Titanic* disaster, the regulators of what can and cannot be done at sea have been playing a catch-up game.

The approach has always been to wait for a problem to develop, then try to find a solution. The trouble with this is that bad practices become well established before they are seen to be a problem. By this time it is often too late, or it has too much impact on shipping operations for corrections to be made.

Take high-speed ferries, for example. These have developed over the past twenty years from a few 30 knot exceptions to whole fleets of very large vessels in full-time service every day running at over 40 knots. Mix these potentially dangerous craft with sailing boats meandering along at single-digit speeds, and disaster is inevitable. But nothing is done because the solution is detrimental to the operation of the fast ferries.

Rigorous examination is needed

What is needed is a much more rigorous examination of new developments as they happen. But where is the expertise to come from to make these assessments? Any such dampener on development in this way is looked upon as hampering progress, and for most investors this is not acceptable.

No, the marine world is a mess and no sector of it is exempt from making it worse. Shipping is under extreme pressure to perform and has turned to technology to find the answers. Fishing is under similar pressure, with a strong emphasis on catch restrictions that add considerably to the stresses and strains on the skipper. Yachting and motorboating are distracted by style and gadgets which take the focus away from sound and sensible design. All around, there is a growing lack of experience, making people less able to cope when things go wrong.

There is no escaping the fact that disasters at sea have not stopped, nor will they stop with the advance of modern technology. With every new concept, the risks increase as the technology is assimilated into current practice. I cannot see any end to things going wrong at sea, nor in history repeating itself.

Disasters at Sea is my small contribution in trying to improve the safety of the marine world.

MAIB

MARINE ACCIDENT INVESTIGATION BRANCH

Narrative

Three crew on board their 11m yacht left their home port in the early morning, having determined that the weather should be good for their intended passage. The wind was south west force 5–6 and good progress was made, the yacht sailing first on a beam reach and then a broad reach. The mainsail had one slab reef taken in, and the roller reefing foresail was also reduced.

Some way into the passage, when the yacht was about 1 mile off a lee shore, the steering wheel mechanism started to make a clicking noise. Soon afterwards, the mechanism jammed completely, leaving the yacht with no steering. The boat gybed, and swung round 180 degrees, through the wind and into a hove-to position with the genoa secured

on the windward side. The crew rigged the emergency tiller, but the rudder would not budge. At this time, the depth of water was 25m, but the yacht only had 20m of anchor chain attached to the anchor.

The crew tried to investigate the steering mechanism further, but at 1350 the skipper decided to make a 'Mayday' call, following which the local lifeboat and SAR helicopter were launched. The yacht drifted inshore, but once in a water depth of 15m, the jib was furled and the anchor let go. Despite using the engine to alleviate the drift, the snatching of the anchor on the bottom caused such loads that the rope connecting the bitter end of the chain to the anchor locker failed and the anchor was lost. With nothing now to restrain it, the yacht continued to drift ashore.

At about 1415, and with the lifeboat in sight, the yacht beached. The lifeboat manoeuvred in close to the shore to try to pass a tow line, but grounded on a small reef.

After freeing itself, the lifeboat stood further offshore and the crew fired a rocket speed line to the yacht. It missed, but a passer-by ashore helped get the speed line to the crew on the yacht, which allowed a tow line to be passed. The tow line was secured and the lifeboat started to pull the yacht off the beach but, unfortunately, the line parted and the yacht beached once again.

At this stage, the lifeboat coxswain decided that the risk to the yacht's crew was too great, and they were evacuated from their vessel by helicopter. The crew suffered no injuries.

The Lessons

1

If your yacht has wheel steering, make sure you are fully conversant with the emergency tiller system. The chances of needing it are probably remote, but solving a steering problem quickly will keep you out of trouble. Pay particular attention to the linkage between the rudder stock and the wheel because, as was the case in this accident, disconnecting the two can be the only way to free the rudder.

2

Be alert to navigational dangers and, where possible, keep well clear of a lee shore. On this occasion, the crew returned to the vessel at low tide to salvage some belongings. The yacht, however, was not salvageable and became a total loss. There is no great need to be sailing 1nm off a very rocky coast. Standing further off will give you extra breathing space to deal with emergencies and the unexpected.

3

Ensure you have sufficient chain and rope attached to your anchor, and that it is of the correct size. For the yacht in this accident, 20m of chain was half the amount recommended. If weight is a major consideration on your yacht, then rope and chain can be used; but ensure you have sufficient chain to assist holding. The prudent mariner will also carry a kedge anchor, which can be used as a back up in an emergency.

Capsize

The horizon was playing tricks and was reluctant to stay still. This was no ordinary rolling of a ship at sea. That horizon wanted to switch from horizontal to vertical. We were very close to capsizing in a big storm in the Atlantic. And we were scared. In Texas, the ship had been loaded with a cargo of grain, one of the most dangerous cargoes you can carry, because it is very fluid and tends to flow from side to side as the ship rolls. To ensure stability, what are called 'shifting boards' were fitted into the ship's holds. These were a kind of temporary longitudinal bulkhead that were intended to limit the flow of grain each way as the ship rolled.

So with our shifting boards in place and a full cargo of grain, we headed out into the Atlantic in the winter. As usual, it was storm after storm on our way across to Europe. The one that did the damage was

The Flying Enterprise *was abandoned by her crew when she started listing. Only the captain remained on board as tugs tried to take her in tow but she eventually sank in the English Channel.*

The car carrier Tricolour *capsized in the Dover Straits after being in a collision and became a serious hazard to shipping, with other vessels hitting the wreck.*

a full force 10, with huge seas running. The noise was the first indication that something was wrong. It was the sound of the shifting boards giving way, allowing the grain to flow unrestricted all to one side. Just what we did not want to happen.

A 30 degree list

Almost immediately, the ship took on a 30 degree list. That would have been scary enough in calm water. In those wild seas, it meant that the ship was rolling over to a frightening 50 or 60 degrees on the low side, and just about coming upright on the return roll. Ships like our 6,000 tonner could normally maintain stability only to around 70 or 80 degrees, so we knew that we were close to rolling over completely. The tension was unbelievable.

Each time the ship rolled over to leeward, it seemed to hover at that steep angle for ever. Then slowly, ever so slowly, it would return to the upright. You held your breath each time the ship rolled and hovered at that crazy slant, thinking it was the end. Would she go this time, or next? The waiting and tension were almost unbearable. We knew that if she went over and capsized, there was little or no hope of survival in the freezing cold waters of the winter Atlantic.

The captain was nursing the ship, trying to find the best heading and speed to limit the rolling.

The ferry Estonia *after she capsized in heavy seas. The liferaft would have inflated automatically when the pressure release system activated.*

We could not shift the cargo back because it would have just returned to the low side again. Filling ballast tanks was also out of the question because the free liquid surface would have made stability even worse. Of course, you couldn't stand this level of tension indefinitely. Amazingly, as the hours passed, life returned to some sort of normality, as you learned to live in a world that was forever tilted so steeply that you could not stand up. We ate, we even slept, and we survived like that for 36 hours before the storm abated enough to try to stabilise the ship. We must have looked a sight as we ran into harbour with our heavy list. But, thank goodness, alive, safe and fairly sound.

That experience was a long drawn-out affair, with the ship threatening to capsize at any moment. We were lucky that it held. There is little chance of escape when a ship capsizes.

Capsize tends to be a very sudden event. Usually it results from something else going wrong, entirely unrelated to the capsize. It tends to be a consequence of an accident rather than the primary cause, although the sudden capsize of fishing boats can be pinned down primarily to an abrupt event out at sea. Modern cargo ships have a considerable history of capsizing in harbour, which suggests that stability – particularly in cargo handling – is not a very exact science, even with the latest technology.

Fishing boats and offshore supply vessels are two of the very few categories of vessel that load and discharge cargoes at sea. A capsize is caused by the vessel losing stability when the forces that normally keep it on an even keel get out of balance. No longer stable, the craft can turn over at any time.

Stability

Of key importance to vessel stability is the location of the centre of gravity. When you shift weight around on board, as the sea did to us with that cargo of grain, or when you add or remove weights, the centre of gravity will move up or down. When it moves too high, the vessel becomes unstable, making a capsize almost inevitable.

When you add weight to a vessel out at sea, you move the centre of gravity up or down, depending on where you add it. Though this certainly affects the inherent stability of the vessel, there is no easy way of predicting exactly how. So a fishing vessel might already have deteriorating stability out at sea as the size of the catch in her holds grows. Then maybe she ships some water on deck from a rough sea, adding even more weight and making her temporarily top-heavy. If that water is slow to drain, stability is slow to recover, and in those critical seconds the fishing boat could easily capsize. This is not an uncommon scenario with smaller fishing boats, where the focus is on catching fish and the skipper pays little attention to the stability of his boat. You might even find that the scuppers have been blocked off to prevent fish draining away with any water that is shipped aboard. With nowhere to go, the water remains on board, ready to overturn the boat at any moment.

This fishing boat is operating in breaking waves – just the sort of conditions where a capsize can occur.

Fishing is a dangerous game

Of course with fishing boats there can be other factors. The trawl can snag on the seabed, exerting a strain on the wire that can pull the boat over, destroying stability and capsizing her. Fishing is very dangerous, and the safety of the vessel relies heavily on the skill and expertise of the skipper. To cope with big and sudden changes at sea, fishing boats are usually built with a big reserve of stability. But those reserves can disappear in a flash when large quantities of water are shipped on deck.

Offshore supply vessels are another type of boat that load and discharge cargo at sea, often in very rough conditions, as they keep the drilling rigs supplied with necessities. Again the risk of capsize is always present, and like fishing boats they are also at risk from a man-made source of danger. Fishing boats, for instance, often have a trawl line out from the side or stern to tow the fishing gear. If this line fouls around something on the seabed, the sudden sharp pull can destabilise the vessel. If this is not countered quickly by using the engines, a capsize is highly likely. Offshore vessels are at similar risk in handling the very heavy anchors and moorings that are used to hold rigs in position. This is what capsized the *Bourbon Dolphin* in the wild waters of the Atlantic, west of the Shetland Islands. Eight crew were lost, but remarkably seven survived despite the winter conditions.

The **Bourbon Dolphin** *operating at an oil drilling rig. These rigs are moored with heavy anchors and it is thought that the capsize occurred when the anchor wire put a heavy side load on the ship in the rough winter conditions.*

Snagging on the bottom

It was reported that the *Bourbon Dolphin* capsized recovering a heavy anchor in what should have been a routine operation. It is not clear whether the anchor was snagged or whether the wire being recovered slipped along the side of the vessel. The ship was reported to be operating in waves of up to 6m in height, considered by some to be outside safe operating limits for this type of operation. As always with this type of event, it is difficult to get a complete picture of what happened. Among those lost was the fifteen-year old son of the captain, who was doing work experience on board.

Stability is rarely a problem in motor yachts, and adequate stability is usually built into the design. Once afloat, very little changes on board, so that the stability level remains with the yacht for the rest of its life. The only changes are when fuel and water are added or used up.

Sailboats, though, are different. They have a heavy keel to balance the heeling effect as the wind presses on the sails, which for most practical purposes works well. There is an inherent safety margin too. As the boat heels to the wind from pressure on the sails, the area of canvas exposed to the wind is reduced by the angle of heel. The yacht naturally lies in equilibrium as wind pressure balances against the slant. With bad luck and severe weather, a yacht can be knocked flat to her beam ends by a violent squall, a mishap known as a knock-down. Even far over and lying on her side, as long as nothing breaks and water does not enter the hull, she will always come back upright again.

Don't lose your keel

This whole balance is completely upset should the keel ever fall off. In the quest for lighter and lighter weight, and higher performance, designers pare the scantlings down to the bone, and there have been notable cases of race boats losing their keels. It has to be said that the keels in question are usually extreme in design, more like a counterbalancing lead weight on the end of a long thin fin. Making such a keel secure enough to withstand the very high stresses of a racing yacht in the open ocean is not easy. As you might expect, high profile cases of keel loss have often occurred after many days at sea, pointing to metal fatigue in the keel supports as a probable cause. Simon LeBon's *Drum* lost its keel in the Western Approaches to the English Channel while Tony Bullimore aboard *Exide Challenger* lost his in the wild depths of the Southern Indian Ocean. Both of these yachts capsized in storm conditions, quickly turning the situation into one of survival. Mike Golding was a bit luckier when his keel dropped off, nearing the end of a Round the World Single-handed race. Golding managed to keep the yacht upright and finish the race, demonstrating that yacht hulls are generally stable without their keels. However, to do so he had to reduce the sail area to just a rag and lost a few places in the final stages of the race – very frustrating, but at least he was still alive.

Multihulls

Multihulls are altogether different in a capsize. They don't have keels to lose, and with the wide spread of their beam they are inherently stable. But in a strong enough burst of wind they can turn over, and once they go, there is no return. Most single-handed ocean races have seen multihull capsizes in which (hopefully) the lone yachtsman gets out on to the upturned hull and waits for rescue. Structural damage to the hull can also lead to capsize, which is always a risk with performance multihulls.

I was navigator on the 80ft catamaran *Chaffoteaux Challenger* when she was attempting an Atlantic sailing record. We did not capsize, but when the hulls started to crack around the cockpit area, we knew that there was a strong possibility that the boat would break in half. We

A capsized trimaran. Because multihulls are just as stable when they are capsized they have no chance of being righted by the crew.

also knew that if that happened, a capsize was likely. Under circumstances like that, there is not a lot you can do except give the boat as easy a ride as possible to reduce the stresses – and make sure everyone has an escape route if the boat turns upside down. On *Chaffoteaux Challenger,* there were hatches in the bottom of the cross beam between the hulls, and in the hull sides themselves. As it turned out, we were rescued before we had to resort to using them.

Survivors cling to the hull of their capsized powerboat, waiting for rescue.

On a cruising multihull, the chances of a capsize are relatively small – but it does happen. You know things are getting close to the limit when the weather hull starts to lift clear of the water. From that point on, there is no more stability. If you want to survive, you either need to bring the boat up into the wind or ease the sails. I am not a big fan of multihulls, partly because the twin structures are much more highly stressed than a monohull. They are also less forgiving, with a much more sudden transition from being OK to near disaster.

Powerboats

You very rarely hear of powerboats capsizing, though they seldom venture out in conditions severe enough for a capsize to occur. The highest risk of a capsize is probably in a following sea, when the boat might broach. This is less likely out in the open sea, where the waves tend to break just near the crest, and there is not the huge rush of white water down the face of the wave that triggers a full scale broach.

Broaching and capsizing is much more likely on a harbour bar, where the waves break in much the same way as they do on a beach. Many fine boats, often lifeboats and fishing boats trying to get back into harbour, have been lost in this way. I have found that deeper draft boats are much less likely to broach in these heavy breaking sea conditions, perhaps because the deep keel is well below the depth of the breaking wave crest, maintaining the boat's directional stability.

A capsized powerboat. There is nothing the crew can do in this situation except await rescue.

Speed and broaching

Broaching will be covered in more detail in the Harbours chapter of this book. However, the higher speed of many powerboats can be a safety factor in following seas, when capsize is a threat. If the boat runs faster than the waves, it is in a position – or at least the driver is – to dictate how it lies in relation to the wave crests. Its very speed reduces the risk of a broaching capsize in stormy seas on open waters.

I am critical of modern lifeboat designs that have a maximum speed of not much more than 20 knots. With barely enough power to run before a big following sea, these lifeboats are at a high risk of broaching as they are overtaken by waves in the open ocean. Of course, slow displacement boats do not have any choice. But at least slow lifeboats have the option of streaming a drogue to reduce the chance of a broach.

When you are operating in extreme conditions, there is always the risk of a capsize. The risks are even higher for lifeboats. They have to help others more than focus on their own survival. However, all modern lifeboats, both fast and slow, are now designed to be self-righting, so that if they do capsize, they come the right way up again. Making the boat do this is really just a question of design, by ensuring that it is unstable when inverted. A bottom-heavy distribution of weights makes sure that the boat will always return to upright.

This rescue boat has an inflatable bag mounted on the frame at the stern. If the boat capsizes, this bag can be inflated to bring the boat back upright again.

Self-righting

It is one thing to make the boat self-righting, but the crew also have to survive the experience. Unless they are firmly strapped into their seats, they can suffer serious injury as the boat turns through 360 degrees. The engine also has to cut out automatically, to avoid damage and be able to start again.

Self-righting is a complex design job, and small RIBs (Rigid Inflatable Boats) used as rescue boats often have an inflatable bag mounted on a frame at the stern to make them self-right. This inflation could be automatic, but the preferred system is manual, to be triggered once the crew are all accounted for, and not trapped under the boat. Though this arrangement is fine, like all self-righting systems it may not work in shallow water when the boat touches the bottom – the very conditions likely to cause a capsize. Most of the capsizes experienced with RNLI RIB rescue boats have occurred coming into a beach, as they slow to make a landing. Following seas that are breaking on your approach are not kind if you slow down. If a wave catches you from behind, over the boat goes.

Pitch-poling

Pitch-poling is another way to capsize – in this case lengthwise, either bow over stern, or more likely, stern over bow. People have done this and lived to tell the tale, but it must be the most frightening experience, and one in which the boat is sure to be damaged quite seriously. If you experience a pitch-pole on a yacht, you are immediately in a pretty serious survival situation. It happens most often when running in a very heavy following sea, with the wind strength going off the scale. Your boat is likely to be running under bare poles, with warps out astern to try to slow it down. Picture the hull rushing down the face of a wave, then burying its bow in the wall of the trough in front, coming to an almost instant dead stop. Still hurtling forward, the stern tries to catch up with the bow – and over she goes, end-over-end.

Running in these conditions in a violent Atlantic storm on *Chaffoteaux Challenger,* I was convinced

Rescuers coming to the aid of a small capsized boat.

we were going to pitch-pole. Even with warps out and no sail, we were still doing 10 knots in a 70 knot wind. It was wild and scary, and I was on deck because I didn't like the idea of being down below if things went wrong. Holding onto the mast was the only way I could stand up in that wind. Suddenly the boat took off like an express train down the face of a monster wave. In the trough, she just kept going down and down, and I found myself up to my chest in water.

This is it, I thought. She's going to pitch-pole. The bows are stopped in the wave, the stern is rushing to overtake them, and the force of the wind on the mast is helping to whip her over.

That would have been the end. My immediate reaction was to hang on like grim death, to avoid being swept overboard. It was an eternity before the bows started to lift. Ever so slowly, she rose and the water drained away, returning my surroundings to some sort of normality. The alternative pitch-pole, when the bow goes over the stern, is more likely to occur in big head seas. The wave face gets near vertical, then starts to break. The pressure of water on the bow could force it right over, although this would probably be in a sort of rolling motion – a combination of pitch-poling and capsize; almost a broach in reverse. Whatever the mechanics of the movement, it must be the most terrifying experience. And in violent seas if it happens once, it can happen a second time. With both capsizes and pitch-poling, crews often report a succession of occurrences.

The damage that a pitch-pole or capsize can inflict on a small craft is not hard to visualise. Between one split-second and another, you are rushing headlong towards disaster. At the very least, anything stowed on deck is likely to be washed away – and that could include your liferaft, together with your chances of survival. Boats, however, are remarkably resilient, and the stories of survival after capsize or pitch-poling are testimony to the fact that horrific though they are, both are survivable. Of course we hear about them from those who lived to tell the tale, rather than the unfortunates who did not make it. There are also cases where the boat has survived, but the crew has not.

Free surface water effect

Damage to a boat that allows water to enter the hull is more likely to lead to a sinking than a capsize. This certainly applies to a yacht, where it's the keel that maintains the stability. It is quite different with a motor-boat, as the 'free surface water effect' inside the hull could easily lead to a capsize. Once water is inside the hull, stability is lost. Motorboats and ships are normally stable to between 50 and 70 degrees of heel. This is the angle at which the boat can lie over and still have enough righting moment to bring it back up again. The limit for that angle, while stability is still positive, is usually when the edge of the deck goes under water. If there is no righting moment at that point, stability deteriorates to zero. When it does, a capsize may be close, or even inevitable.

That free surface water effect can change stability in an instant. Exactly like the grain cargo that nearly caused us to capsize on the *Marjarta*, but with shipboard water slopping unchecked inside the low side of the vessel, adding treacherously to the list. The danger with a free water surface is that if the vessel is rolling, the water inside the hull will surge from side to side, adding more weight to its momentum, worsening the angle of heel with every roll – and so causing a capsize.

Any liquid moving to and fro like this is a danger, which is why shipboard fuel and water tanks are divided up so as not to stretch the full width of the ship. Under normal circumstances, everything is fine. But when a free water surface gets out of control, as can happen on the full-width car deck of a Ro-Ro ferry, or simply when water on a deck surface has nowhere to drain away, then the vessel is in danger.

The *Herald of Free Enterprise* disaster is testimony to the hazards of a free water surface. Water entered the bow doors of the ferry, which had not been closed before leaving harbour. When the ship heeled into a turn, the water surged to one side, causing the ship to capsize, with severe loss of life to passengers and crew. Perhaps it was fortunate that the capsize occurred in relatively shallow water. On her side on a sandbar, the capsized ship was still partially above water, allowing a greater number of survivors to escape. Even so, with 179 dead, the capsize was a major shipping disaster. Findings at the official inquiry eventually led to significant design and operational changes.

This is a prime case of inherent dangers only being recognised after major loss of life. There had been similar capsizes of Ro-Ro cargo ships prior to the *Herald of Free Enterprise* disaster. But capsizes for cargo vessels do not attract the same publicity as capsizes of passenger ships. Furthermore, many of these cargo ship capsizes occurred in harbour, so the risks were not the same as they were at sea. I had an article published about the possibility of a sudden rollover just like the *Herald of Free Enterprise* a year before it happened. I even used a photo of her sister ship to illustrate my point. But as always, it took a disaster before anyone paid any heed – and in this case, the loss of 179 lives to underline it.

You can easily imagine how the movement of a free water surface could cause a ship to capsize at sea. The stability might be further reduced by collision damage to the hull. Or, as in the case of the *Al Salam Boccaccio* while crossing the Red Sea, from the weight of water used to fight a fire on the car deck.

Capsize berthed alongside

So far, we have considered capsizes that happen at sea. Now how, you might ask, can a ship possibly capsize in port, especially when berthed alongside a dock? There have been several cases where this has occurred; one of the most recent involved the Ro-Ro container ship *Republica di Genova* in the port of Antwerp. Though

Ro-Ro ships can become unstable when they are loading or discharging cargo. This is the **Republica di Genova,** *which capsized in Antwerp Docks in Belgium.*

still under investigation, the most likely cause of this capsize appears to be discharging ballast tanks at the same time as loading cargo. This is actually regular practice, done to keep the ship on an even keel during loading, and to maintain the stern Ro-Ro ramp at the right height. As already seen, when a tank is half-full, there is a free surface water effect even when it is subdivided and this can easily surge to one side unless ballasting is carefully controlled. Once the ship heels to a certain angle, more water can come in through the bow or stern doors, dragging the ship further over onto her beam ends. The same week that the *Republica di Genova* capsized, another Grimaldi Lines ship (the *Republica di Venecia)*, was in a collision in the North Sea Canal while running up to Amsterdam. Not a good week for Messrs Grimaldi, or their insurers!

Container ships

Stability can be a serious problem for container ships. The *Dongedijk* capsized while manoeuvring in the Suez Canal because its container cargo had not been loaded correctly. In 2000, the *Han Se* suffered a similar fate in South Korea. And again in 2001, a container ship capsized because the ballasting was carried out incorrectly during a heavy cargo lift. Heavy-lift ships are particularly vulnerable, regularly handling super-hefty cargo items of up to 1,500 tons. Another cause of capsize for container ships is when the declared weight of cargo loaded in containers is deliberately falsified to reduce shipping costs. Heavier than declared, these containers can seriously affect the vessel's trim and, put on top of the deck stack, they can be disastrous.

Apart from Ro-Ro vessels, most capsizes involve ships damaged in a collision or from grounding, or being overloaded. Cargo ships usually have well-divided hulls, so that there is less risk of capsize from compartments flooding. However, a lot of smaller coasting ships have just a single long, open hull. Should this ever be pierced, there could very quickly be a large open water surface in the hold.

Passenger ships are bound by tighter rules. If holed, a typical liner should be able to remain afloat with at least two-compartments flooded. This rule is designed to keep the ship afloat and reasonably upright in the event of a collision. Modern thinking is that in an emergency, such as a fire or sustaining hull damage, the ship herself should be a refuge and means of escape. The evidence, though, demonstrates that this may not be enough.

The *Achille Lauro* met the two-compartment requirement, but towards the end of her voyage was reported to be less than normally stable because fuel from bunkers in the bottom of the ship had been used up. After the ship was holed in a collision, without its weight as ballast, a list developed which allowed water to run over the top of further watertight bulkheads, making the ship unstable.

It was said that the *Titanic* was unsinkable. Even with all our technology, there is still no such thing as an unsinkable ship. A ship's stability is threatened if the hull is ever damaged in any way, a very real risk with the high-sided (and top-heavy) modern passenger ships. They might meet the standards demanded by regulations, but are they well-found enough to prevent disaster?

Back in the 1950s, an American cargo ship famously hit the headlines when she developed a list in the Western Approaches. The ex-Liberty ship *Flying Enterprise* first took on the list when her cargo shifted, just as we experienced aboard the *Marjarta*. Except for the captain, her crew were taken off, leaving the ship to drift as the list increased and more of her holds flooded. A rescue tug, the *Turmoil,* was sent to her aid, and several attempts were made to pass a line to the ship, now almost on her beam ends. The saga went on for days. In worsening weather, the ship's captain was too fatigued to secure the heavy tow rope, and the mate of the *Turmoil* actually leaped across to help as the two vessels crashed together in heavy seas. It was to no avail. The ship settled lower in the water, and the two men were taken off just before she turned turtle and sank. It was a heroic fight, but as so often happens, the sea claimed victory.

Safe under all conditions?

Trying to design a ship that will remain upright and afloat in all possible emergency conditions is a difficult task. The safety demands would severely compromise the everyday performance of the ship, and there would still be the human failings of alarms not working, scuppers blocked, or other negligence. To be 'safe', any ship depends on everything working satisfactorily. Ensuring her crew are always diligent is a big assumption to make.

One issue needing urgent attention is small craft hull integrity, where subdivisions are rare and damage protection is minimal. So often you read reports of water flooding into a hull, the crew helpless, and the boat sinking. Held upright by the keel, a yacht taking water is unlikely to capsize. Not so a powered boat, with its hull-shell of wide open, uninterrupted space. Nobody wants a luxury yacht split up by watertight subdivisions that restrict movement about the boat. However, it should be possible to build in double bottom tanks, which would at least offer some protection in a grounding or collision. Usually there is a watertight bulkhead between the engine room and the rest of the boat, and another in the bow, often known as the 'collision bulkhead'. Neither of these is really enough, and collision bulkhead rarely extends down below the waterline. So while it might offer some protection, it does nothing if the boat runs aground, even though damage to the hull at the bow is likely to be underwater. This lack of protection is strange when you consider this is a common type of accident, and that by preventing the hull from flooding you have a good chance of avoiding either a capsize or a sinking.

Capsize while racing

Capsizing is spectacular for spectators, especially with offshore racing boats. These boats rely on a lot of air lift between their dual hulls to improve efficiency, and the drivers' skill is in balancing this air lift against the powerful engine thrust, so the boat rides level and true at very high speeds. Get it wrong and the results can be dramatic, the boat lifting at the bow and flipping right over before landing upside down. In one sequence, filmed in the Middle East, the boat actually flew backwards for three metres above the water before landing with a big splash. Perhaps this technique is a new way of 'flying' over sandbanks instead of going round them. Unfortunately, the landing technique is still not perfected enough to keep racing. Though these are dramatic incidents, the crews survive

Offshore racing powerboats can capsize dramatically when the air lift under the hull causes the boat to become unstable and flip over.

because they are strapped into a safety capsule. It gives them an escape route through the bottom of the hull, as well as a temporary air supply.

Racing RIBs capsize differently. At super high speed, very little of a fast boat hull is actually in the water. There was one particular RIB that started to bounce from one inflatable tube to the other as it heeled first left and then right as the driver flicked the steering wheel. There was one final bounce before the boat flipped right over.

This might sound extreme and remote from day-to-day boating. Fortunately, capsizes are rare and few people have any experience of them. Unless of course you are one of those unfortunate few, and find yourself adrift on a liferaft – a type of craft particularly vulnerable to capsizing. Adrift on a liferaft in severe conditions, people face further hardship as their raft capsizes on them. I cannot imagine anything worse than escaping with your life into a raft, braving storms and worse, and then having the thing itself turn over. Not only have you lost precious equipment but you also face the Herculean task of righting the raft. You are wet and cold, and it's difficult to climb back aboard. Very often, this is the challenge that tips the scales. You are too mentally and physically exhausted to cope any longer. Trying to right a liferaft in a swimming pool on a training course was the nearest I ever got to such a challenge, and that was difficult enough.

Of course, small craft capsizes are not restricted to racing. All kinds of other power and sail categories are trying to push the limits. The capsizing risks aboard cruising yachts are relatively small, even in extreme conditions, although there is a new breed of long-range cruising motor yacht that may find its stability tested in extreme conditions. These new designs are not self-righting in the event of a capsize, and I sense a question mark over their abilities in very heavy sea conditions. As their owners seek more extreme adventures, the risks will get higher.

Overloaded boats

The risk of capsize is even greater with the dramatic increase in migrants undertaking perilous ocean voyages to find a new life in developed countries. Most of them are from parts of North Africa en route to the Canary Islands, Spain, Malta and Italy. The voyages can take several days, often in unsuitable and very overloaded boats. Add in some even mildly adverse weather and disaster can strike. Run only for profit, most boats have little in the way of safety and survival equipment. Should they ever fill with water and capsize from overloading, the loss of life can be frightening.

Worse, because these voyages are mostly unrecorded until the boat arrives at its destination, actual losses of migrant boats are never fully known. Nor are migrants any safer should their boats be intercepted by patrols near destination coastlines. One such vessel, with over 100 people on board, capsized in a big wave when a coastguard boat was alongside, and over 50 people were drowned. Nor is this an isolated case, so it is likely that migrant boats will increasingly feature in the casualty lists as the trade increases.

Among full-size ships, if you look at the statistics, the risk of capsize does seem to be decreasing. Though it might seem profitable to reduce this risk of collision etc, there is still the factor of human error, for which a solution has yet to be found.

Another major cause of capsize is from tackling a fire on board with water pumped from the sea. Introducing water into the hull always brings the risk of generating a free surface water effect. Both the French liner *Normandie* and the original *Queen Elizabeth* were lost to shipboard fires in this way. At least a capsize does succeed in putting the fire out, though it is not a logical way to promote safety!

MARINE ACCIDENT INVESTIGATION BRANCH

Young woman killed when day boat capsizes

A group of 15 people were on a week-long activity based team-building course organised by the Prince's Trust in Slough. As part of the course, the group of 12 volunteers and three team leaders/assistants undertook a day's sailing in Milford Haven led by five instructors employed by the Trust.

The group left Neyland Marina at about 1230 on 3 February in four 6.1m Explorer II ketch-rigged open day boats. Each had five people on board, at least one of whom was an instructor. The boats were rigged and equipped with an outboard motor, crutches and oars.

The weather was fine with a moderate westerly breeze. The outboard motors were used for the first part of the day to enable the volunteers to gain experience in boat handling. After a picnic lunch the crews in two of the boats motored across the Haven to Carr Flats where they prepared to sail back to the marina.

The mizzen sail was hoisted on one of the boats as she motored slowly into wind. While preparing to set the jib some water washed over the port gunwale, prompting the crew to move quickly to starboard to avoid getting wet. The boat heeled to starboard and started to ship water. The situation was possibly aggravated by wind filling the mizzen sail. The boat capsized.

The instructor and volunteers were thrown into the water. The instructor attempted to right the boat but, after lying on its side for a few moments, it inverted. As it did so one of the crutches possibly snagged the buoyancy aid of one of the volunteers, a young woman, who had found herself between the two masts. She

was pulled down and held underwater beneath the upturned hull. As the boat inverted the centreboard slid into its housing, frustrating further attempts to right it. Despite strenuous and prolonged attempts by two instructors (the other boat had come to their assistance) they were unable to free the victim.

The accident was witnessed from the beach by two fishermen who ran to their boat and set off a distress rocket. A harbour authority launch came to assist and managed to attach a line to the rigging and right the boat. As it came upright the unconscious woman slipped out of her buoyancy aid and began to float away. One of the instructors began in-water mouth-to-mouth resuscitation. She was recovered to an inflatable boat which had also come to their assistance and resuscitation attempts continued as she was taken ashore to a waiting ambulance. Despite their efforts they were unable to save her.

The Lessons

1

The boats had been modified to enable them to be rowed. The crutches were mounted through the gunwale capping outboard of the hull and were secured with splitpins. This made their shipping and removal slow and awkward and it had become the accepted practice to leave them permanently in place. By leaving them in situ, the crutches had become a snagging hazard for mooring lines, sheets and other rigging. They were vulnerable when coming alongside pontoons or other craft and people could fall or trip over them. They could also snag clothing or lifejackets in the event of

a capsize. Crutches should always be
unshipped when not in use.

2

Explorer II, like many open day boats of similar size,
is neither a very stable keel boat nor a light buoyant
dinghy. Such boats can and will, on occasions,
capsize.

3

Open day boats, unlike lighter dinghies, are
difficult to right by the crew if they capsize. Some
have a tendency to invert, which makes righting
them even more awkward without assistance from
another craft.

4

Distributing weight evenly for the conditions is part
of sailing and novices must be briefed about what
to expect and what to avoid. From time to time
water will be shipped and people will get wet.
They must expect this.

5

As part of the investigation an Explorer II was
capsized intentionally. When inverted, she sank
slowly by the stern. This was because the aft
stowage lockers were not watertight. When she
was righted the water level in the cockpit was
above the top of the outboard engine well and
made bailing impossible. Other open day boats
share this characteristic and appropriate measures
should be taken to provide additional buoyancy.
Such measures should also include providing a
means of buoyancy on the mast to prevent
inversion in the event of a capsize.

6

Before purchasing a boat, look for the European
Standards plate marked CE which will provide
information on loading and power limitations.

Fire

Fire at sea can be very frightening because there is nowhere to escape except into a liferaft or lifeboat and that can be a big risk. This burnt-out pleasure boat shows how destructive fire can be.

Fire

It is more than likely that if something is to go wrong at sea, it will happen in the dead of night. I was on watch at three in the morning; we had rounded Land's End and the Lizard Point, and were now set for a clear run up the English Channel. I started to relax; the dangerous reef of rocks that stretches out from the Lizard was now behind us. There was nothing in sight ahead, and behind, the bright flashes of the Lizard lighthouse were illuminating the wheelhouse. It was then that the visibility started to deteriorate.

Smoke

It was only when the lights on the dashboard became fuzzy that I realised the visibility problem was inside, not outside, the wheelhouse. Then came the smell, and I quickly realised that it was smoke: pungent, foul-smelling smoke that was filling the wheelhouse. We were on fire and my first thought was to get outside, away from the poisonous-smelling fumes. After a few gulps of fresh air I realised that the rest of the crew were down below. Holding my breath, I rushed down to rouse them from their slumbers. My shouts of 'Fire' were met with disbelief until the first wisps of smoke found their way below, galvanising the crew out of the wheelhouse in a rush.

It was time to take action. There was no sign of flames and the problem seemed to lie within the

Help has come to this vessel, which has a major fire on board. Outside assistance can often arrive too late to have much effect on a boat fire out at sea.

wheelhouse. Closer inspection with a torch showed smoke escaping between the cracks in the deckhead panelling, but why? The problem seemed to be the electrics, so my first thought was to turn off the main battery isolating switch. This had no effect. Taking it in turns to gulp a breath of fresh air and then rush below, we began the task of ripping out the deckhead panelling to get to the seat of the fire. As each panel came down there was a burst of flame as oxygen reached the fire, creating more of those poisonous fumes. Each flare was doused with a burst from a fire extinguisher and finally we seemed to have the situation under control.

It had been a tense half hour, with the boat drifting around on idle before we got things under control. It transpired that the fire had started with a short circuit in a wire that ran directly to the batteries, bypassing the main switch. This wire fed the anchor light, hence the decision to bypass the batteries, but with dangerous consequences. The constant movement at sea had caused the insulation to break down and triggered a short circuit. It was the foam plastic insulation behind the panelling that had caught fire and produced the noxious fumes.

It was time to head into the nearest port (Falmouth) and get sorted out, but when we checked our position, we were just a few hundred yards off the end of the Lizard lifeboat slipway. Had we needed to call for help, and we came very close that night, the lifeboat could have hit us as it cleared the slipway! Even with help so close at hand we were fortunate not to have needed it.

Danger from water

Fire at sea is terrifying; there is nowhere to run and little firefighting equipment on board. Despite being surrounded by the best firefighting medium, water, a boat lacks the correct equipment to deliver it. Assuming it is possible to get the water to the fire, excess fluid on board can prove hazardous. Not only will the boat get lower in the sea, but the free water surface will affect the vessel's stability. While sinking

Here a tug with firefighting monitors is trying to extinguish a fire on a barge.

or capsizing will certainly extinguish the fire, it will also leave the crew with only one option: the liferaft, assuming it is not on fire as well.

Today, it would be reasonable to assume that all potentially combustible materials are removed from ships and boats, but this simply isn't practical. Materials such as the insulation foam in the motor cruiser fire described earlier would not find a place on a modern vessel, but there are a thousand other combustible items that would: clothing, personal effects, food, drink, and indeed most of the things that make life bearable on board. Then, of course, there is the fuel. Although fuel is contained in tanks, it must come into the engine room at some point, and it only takes a small leak for a fire to start. Engine rooms are one of the most common locations for fires onboard, and fuel is often the cause. Cargo ships and Ro-Ro ferries carry the added risk from their cargo. Loads such as liquid and pressurised gas or highly flammable fuels pose not only a fire hazard, but also an explosion risk. The undeclared (and possibly dangerous) contents of containers are the most worrying risk of all.

Cargo is not often the cause

Strangely, it is rarely the type of cargo that is the primary cause of a fire, although coal cargoes still present a hazard. Coal can lie smouldering for weeks in the hold of a ship; it is only when the hatches are removed and oxygen is added that the fire comes to life. Fortunately, such fires almost invariably occur in port (when the hatches are opened) and can be dealt with by the fire services. Hosing down the fire helps to keep things cool; it is then a question of getting the coal or its remains out of the hold. In a recent case

Ships coming to the aid of a vessel on fire can put themselves at risk. This is a fire on a bulk carrier with a cargo of coal. It is extremely difficult to cope with this type of fire.

a coal cargo fire had spread to all the holds of a ship at anchor off Singapore. The salvors involved did not dare open the hatches. They attempted to inject CO_2 into the holds, but eventually the only solution was to deliberately ground the vessel and flood the holds with water. It took nearly a month to complete the whole operation.

The cause of many serious explosions on tankers is often not the cargo, which can be inert when the tanks are full, but the gas that forms when the tanks are empty. In the past, there have been serious explosions when cargo tanks have been cleaned with water sprays and static electricity generated from these sprays has ignited the gas in the hold. Today, cargo tanks are filled with an inert gas that prevents the formation of an explosive gas mixture. Paradoxically, this inert safety gas also poses a hazard, as the crew must wear breathing apparatus when entering the space to check the success of a cleaning operation. Should tankers collide, there is always the risk of a fire. While the collision itself is serious enough, it is often the resulting fire that leads to loss of life. There have been many horrific cases of tanker fires in the past, but enhanced technology and better understanding of the causes have improved the situation. Double-hull tankers have not only reduced the risk of hull penetration if the ship grounds, thus avoiding pollution, but have also reduced the risk of fire in a collision.

We seem to have moved away from the dramatic tanker fires that hit the headlines a decade or two ago. These days many of the tanker fires reported involve smaller tankers and chemical carriers, ships that

The burnt-out remains of a ship that has suffered a major superstructure fire.

carry more specialised cargoes, many of them highly inflammable or dangerous. A study has shown that human error is the largest cause of on-board fires or explosions when handling the cargo or managing systems. The procedures for the safe handling of these cargoes are often complex and require special training, but it is still when the tanks are empty or being cleaned that the explosions occur.

Gasoline

Carrying a cargo of gasoline is not something to undertake lightly and the 45,000-tonne tanker, *Quetzalcoal*, had almost finished discharging her gasoline cargo when a massive explosion occurred. Built in 1979, the single-hulled tanker was undergoing repairs during the discharge, which seems a risky venture and raises the question: was the explosion triggered by a welding spark? Eight people died in that catastrophe. It could be argued that a tanker of that age should not have been carrying a cargo of highly inflammable and explosive gasoline. One also wonders if an older ship with a dangerous cargo would attract

The remains of an enclosed lifeboat that was damaged by fire, showing that even the escape boats can be vulnerable.

a high-calibre crew to man it. Interestingly, statistics suggest that fires are not perceived as a major problem in shipping. Only 122 incidents were reported from a total fleet of around 90,000 ships in one year. However, what is significant is that the vast majority of reported incidents occurred in older ships, with 55% occurring in vessels more than 20 years old.

Methanol can be as hazardous a load as gasoline, and the 17,000-tonne tanker *Vicuna* exploded in Brazil when discharging its methanol cargo. As is often the case, the cause of the explosion is not clear, but it resulted in four people dying. It took 24 hours to extinguish the blaze and the ship was split in two.

Executing an escape from a tanker that is on fire can pose a serious threat to the crew. It may be possible to lower the lifeboats, but what if they are lowered into a pool of burning oil on the sea? Fortunately, modern tanker lifeboats now come in the form of a fully enclosed fireproof boat, which should give the crew a chance to escape to a point of safety. Even this is tenuous, as it depends on the lifeboat surviving the fire or explosion intact, and upon its engine starting. It must be a horrific situation: options for escape fast disappearing and little in the way of help from outside sources.

If the risks for the crews of modern tankers seem bad, imagine how much worse it must have been in the days of the early steamships. The 300ft SS *Amazon* was the largest wooden steamer of her time but wooden hulls and boiler fires are not a happy combination. When the ship caught fire in the Bay of Biscay her troubles were only just beginning. The fire could not be controlled and the engine room was

39

abandoned, but the ship was still steaming at full speed. This forced the flames aft, where the passengers had congregated. In an act of incredible bravery, the captain swung the ship around so that the flames engulfed the bridge where he stood. Some lifeboats were launched, but only 58 of the 162 people on board survived.

The requirements for safe carriage of cargoes have been carefully worked out. Provided the correct criteria are maintained, the cargo is essentially safe. However, in the event of major catastrophes these safety standards cannot guarantee safety, especially in the event of a collision where cargo spaces are penetrated. Thankfully, collisions leading to a major fire or explosion are rare. One of the happy consequences of environmental concern is that ships carrying dangerous cargoes have been made safer to reduce pollution, which also decreases the risk of a major fire or explosion.

A patrol boat watches as a tanker fire rages in the USA. Although tanker safety has improved, fires are still a major hazard on these ships with dangerous cargoes.

The wind can be a hazardous addition to the problems of firefighting.

Containers

The emphasis on the occurrence of cargo ship fires seems to have shifted away from tankers to other vessels, such as container ships and Ro-Ro ships. On these vessels the cargo may be much more varied, and with less control over what is in the containers it comes as no surprise that fires are a relatively common occurrence. In theory, the contents of every container should be carefully listed and anything that might constitute a hazardous cargo must be declared. In practice, experts suspect the high costs of shipping a potentially dangerous cargo encourages them to be shipped undeclared. Hazardous cargoes should be stowed at the top of the stack where access is easy, as it can be a real problem on a container ship when one container catches alight near the bottom of the stack. Just getting into a container to reach the seat of the fire may be impossible, and the heat can allow the fire to spread quickly to adjacent containers. There have been cases where a fire starting in just one container has spread throughout the whole cargo and the ship has had to be abandoned.

The recent fire in the large container ship *Hyundai Fortune* shows just how this can happen. The fire was thought to have started in a container holding fireworks that was stowed on deck, but some experts suggest that this was a secondary cause of the fire. They believe the contents of another container actually started the blaze. As the flames spread throughout the ship, the crew were evacuated and salvors fought for days to stabilise the vessel and extinguish the fires. Although taken to a safe anchorage and its undamaged containers discharged, the ship was a total loss, with the value of ship and cargo put in the region of $300 million.

Similarly, the fire on the *Hanjin Pennsylvania* was reported to have started in a container of undeclared dangerous cargo when the ship was south of Sri Lanka, on a voyage to Europe. In this case the fire spread slowly and four days later resulted in a second explosion from containers that were filled with magnesium ingots. A huge fire took hold and the crew wisely abandoned ship. The vessel was towed into harbour and declared a total loss, although she was later refurbished and sent back into service. When the container ship CMA *Djakarta* had a fire in one of her holds when off the coast of Egypt, a novel system of firefighting was used. Helicopters carrying bags full of water flew over the ship, dropping water directly into the hold. The method was successful, but not before much of the cargo had been destroyed.

An example of the way that cargoes can be wrongly labelled was seen many years ago on a ferry in Scandinavia. The cargo on a truck was declared as 'camping equipment', seemingly harmless, and was thus allowed on the passenger ferry. However, shortly after the truck disembarked it was involved in a serious road collision that resulted in a major fire and explosions. The declared 'camping equipment' cargo was in fact a full load of fully charged gas cylinders for camping cooking stoves. This should have been declared as a dangerous cargo, and as such would not have been permitted on a passenger ferry, so it is easy to see the motivation for the vague declaration of the truck's contents.

Another example of disaster with hazardous cargo was seen when the cruise ship *Norwegian Dream* collided with the 52,000-tonne container ship, *Ever Decent* (see the Collision chapter). The containers on the *Ever Decent* held hazardous cargoes that led to a fire on board after the collision. While the collision was dramatic and hit the headlines, the fire was seen as the less serious consequence, but it does demonstrate how one disaster can lead to another with very different consequences. The *Norwegian Dream* was lucky to escape the fire, as some of the containers stowed on the deck of the *Ever Decent* ended up in the bow of the *Norwegian Dream* in an 'exchange' of cargoes during the collision.

The fire on the tanker *Limbourg* was caused by a terrorist attack when the ship was at the southern end of the Red Sea. A small boat packed with explosives was driven into the side of the ship and the subsequent fire raged out of control for days, rendering the ship a total loss. The USS *Cole* suffered a similar fate in the nearby port of Aden.

This phenomenon of terrorist attacks on shipping is yet another danger to be added to the long list of potential disasters at sea. There can never be enough rules and regulations to take into account the risk of terrorist activity, and ships will always be vulnerable to this type of attack.

This fishing boat is well and truly on fire from bow to stern; this is the time to stop fighting the fire and try to escape.

Other vessels are not always equipped to stop a fire; but this military vessel was fitted with a fire monitor to help with this fishing boat fire.

Dangerous cargoes

So far, the world has avoided a major disaster involving a ship with a liquid natural gas cargo. In the event of a cargo tank penetration, this heavier than air gas would mix explosively with the cold sea water. Initially this would cause a pressure explosion as the liquid turned to gas, rupturing the other tanks on the ship and rapidly escalating towards a major disaster. The released gas could then spread out from the ship and on ignition could result in an extensive fire, devastating the ship and anything around it. Therefore it is understandable that other vessels give liquefied natural gas (LNG) ships a very wide berth, and that they have LNG printed on the hull in large letters for quick identification. The transport of liquid gas, whether super cooled as in the case of LNG, or under pressure as in the case of liquefied petroleum gas (LPG), is growing rapidly as the world's consumption of gas as a fuel increases. Thus disaster of this kind is likely to remain an ever increasing danger.

Fires do happen on these ships. Imagine what it must have been like on board the liquid gas carrier, *Linda Kosan*. This 2,223-tonne ship had loaded 320 tonnes of propane and 640 tonnes of butane and was on passage down the English Channel when, on servicing the cargo-cooling compressor, there was an explosion and fire in the compressor room on deck. That fire must have been a terrifying experience considering the 1,000 tonnes of liquid gas on board, but the crew were successful in extinguishing it. Most people (including me) would have launched the lifeboat and run away before disaster struck, but that crew did an amazing job, which provides hope that these crews are well-trained and competent.

Explosion and fire

Fire is one thing on a ship or a boat, but explosions tend to be more sudden and more damaging. Explosions are most likely in the engine room, where diesel fuel under high pressure can leak and, once mixed with the surrounding air, create a blast.

I experienced this on a tramp ship when I first went to sea over 50 years ago. We were steaming along at night, in the middle of the ocean, when there was a sudden and enormous bang. The apprentices' cabin was right above the engine room and it felt as though we were lifted bodily from our bunks. Rushing out we discovered that there was thick black smoke rising from the engine room skylight and below we could see flames. It was a heart-stopping moment. The explosion had taken place in the crank case where an explosive mixture of oil and oxygen had built up. There was no real lasting damage, but it was frightening while it lasted.

Fire can also be caused by a collision, even on leisure vessels.

Engine room fires

Engine room fires are one of the major causes of blazes on board fishing boats. It is interesting to note that the figure given for fires on page 39 does not include fishing boat fires. A quick check through the casualty pages of *Fishing News International* shows around four fires reported every month and these are only the major fires. There must be many smaller fires that go unreported and it has to be said that fishing boats do have a rather casual attitude to safety. Take the case of the British fishing boat that suffered two fires in a two-week period, the second of which led to the vessel flooding and subsequently foundering. In the first fire, smoke was seen coming from the engine compartment and the skipper attempted to operate the CO_2 smothering system, but without closing the ventilation openings. The CO_2 system failed to operate (through poor maintenance) but the fire went out anyway and the vessel was towed in.

The remains of a burnt-out motor cruiser where the superstructure has been completely destroyed.

There is not much hope of salvaging anything from a fishing boat that is alight from stem to stern.

After a major overhaul and with a revitalised CO_2 system, the vessel put to sea again only to experience another engine room fire. This time the CO_2 system was effective, but the fire had damaged a plastic seawater pipe so the vessel flooded and then foundered.

Big fishing boats are not immune and in the United States a factory ship processing fish suffered an engine room fire and had to be towed back to harbour. Off the coast of Chile, 11 crew lost their lives in a major fire on board another factory trawler. This fire started in the packing area but quickly spread. One hundred and sixteen crew abandoned ship and were picked up, but those who lost their lives were thought to have been overcome by the dense fumes from the fire. The insulating foam around the refrigerated spaces on fishing boats can be a major source of toxic fumes, as I discovered with that motor cruiser that caught fire off the Lizard. Once these fumes spread through the vessel, it is a major problem. Not only can the crew be overcome, but their capability to fight the fire can be severely restricted.

Once a fire takes hold it may be impossible to stop.

Fires on small craft

On small craft, and most leisure craft, it is the hot exhaust system that can lead to fires. On the majority of diesel engines up to 3,000 or 4,000hp, the exhaust pipe is injected with the engine cooling water after it has done its job cooling the engine. This serves to get rid of the water via the exhaust and it also serves to cool the exhaust, which would otherwise be red hot. Should the cooling water flow stop, the first indication of a problem is likely to be a red hot exhaust pipe – and possibly a fire. The fire would probably start in the flexible rubber section of the exhaust where the cooling action of the seawater is vital. However, an exhaust fire may not be the worst of the problems, as the interruption of the cooling water flow could be because of a fractured inlet pipe, so not only will the boat possibly be on fire but it could also be sinking. One will eventually stop the other but that will leave you quickly launching the liferaft. This shows how the snowball effect of a single disaster can quickly escalate into something much more serious.

In a case like this the fire would be the second stage of the impending disaster, and this is often the case with disasters at sea. Years ago, when I was working with Trinity House on their lighthouse tenders, we saw smoke rising from a vessel about a mile away as we entered Harwich Harbour. We launched a boat to investigate and came across a 20ft open boat that was on fire from stem to stern. The immensely relieved owner was about to jump overboard when we picked him up.

The fire on this sport fishing boat off the coast of Maine in the USA started with a short circuit. It quickly spread to the rest of the boat.

We enquired about the cause of the fire and were surprised to hear that it was steering failure! Not understanding how steering failure could cause a fire and wondering about this man's sanity, I asked him to explain. 'My boat had wire and pulley steering, where wires leading from the steering wheel to the rudder run over pulleys to pull the tiller in the desired direction. One of the wires broke where it ran around a pulley and the loose end of the wire fell across the open battery terminals and caused a short circuit. I didn't have a fire extinguisher or any means of putting out the fire, which quickly took hold, and I was sure glad to see you guys arrive.' By now the boat had burnt down to the waterline and shortly afterward it sank.

Batteries

Batteries have a huge amount of latent power stored in them and a direct short circuit can quickly get a fire started. I once did surveys on fishing boats and yachts; it is surprising how many boats do not have the battery properly secured. Any movement of the battery can lead to stress on the main battery cables, and once sparks begin fire is not far away.

On one fishing boat I found the main batteries unsecured and simply resting on a ledge. I mentioned this in my report, stating the boat was not safe in its present condition. The owner ignored this and went to sea without taking any corrective action. Sure enough, when the boat encountered rough sea, the batteries slid off the ledge and were short circuited by the steel structure of the hull. The boat went up in flames rapidly. You might wonder how a steel boat can catch fire, but as already mentioned there are many combustible materials on a boat. Once the fire takes hold, plastic pipes start to melt and all the furnishings and fixtures burn. The chances are the boat will either sink or at the very least become a burnt-out wreck.

The crew of a 12m steel-hulled yacht on a passage off the west coast of Scotland were forced to abandon ship after it caught fire. Due to light winds the yacht was motor sailing when the crew noticed smoke coming out around the companionway. On lifting the step, there were flames from the starboard side of the engine around the wiring loom. An extinguisher seemed to put the fire out and the engine was still running, so the voyage continued with the skipper trying to effect repairs. Next, flames were seen coming from a locker and the situation was rapidly getting out of hand. The skipper decided to abandon ship, probably a wise move to get out while they still could. A passing boat picked up the crew and the lifeboat took the yacht in tow, but the interior was almost completely destroyed.

An old wooden sailboat cruising in the same area suffered an explosion after a petrol leakage. The engine was one of those old units that is started on petrol and then switches over to paraffin. The owner reported having had trouble with the engine and it seems that petrol was leaking from the carburettor when under sail. When the starter motor was pressed, up she went. The couple on board were lucky to escape with only minor injuries. It must come as a major shock when such an explosion occurs – one minute you are sailing along enjoying the view, the next your world is in turmoil. Two comments after this disaster were that the fire extinguishers were useless and the bow of the inflatable dinghy was holed (fortunately, it got them ashore safely on the remaining intact compartment).

Petrol fires

The suddenness and disorientation created by a petrol explosion must be similar to that experienced after a lightning strike. Not only is a lightning strike likely to start a fire on board, but it will also destroy all the boat's electronics so communication with the outside world is impossible. Both of these events highlight the need to have the liferaft in a position where it is both easily accessible and least likely to get damaged. Another priority should be a hand-held VHF so that contact can be made should the electrics fail. With explosions likely to start from the engine compartment or down below, stowing the liferaft on the coachroof is probably best, but there is no way to guarantee its survival in a disaster. In any case, in the event of a fire, a liferaft may not be the best option. It will be difficult to move away from the burning craft except downwind, and that may not be the safest escape route when the flames and smoke are also blowing downwind. An inflatable dinghy should provide better mobility and the ability to manoeuvre away from the craft before something explodes.

It is important to exit the burning vessel as early as possible. As already mentioned, the position of a liferaft is critical in the event of a fire, more so than with any other emergency. It all relates to the way a boat will lie on the water when it has stopped. A sailboat is likely to lie across the wind or with the bow heading slightly downwind, although if the sails are still up there is no way of telling how it might end up. The usual stowage location on the coachroof should allow for the liferaft to be launched on either side and it will be clear of the cockpit, where the fire is most likely to start.

A powerboat will generally lie with its stern into the wind. This means that a fire in the engine compartment at the stern is likely to spread quickly into the rest of the boat if there is a breeze to fan the flames. On a high-sided boat the only launching and boarding place for the liferaft may be at the stern, which means that after the launch the raft will be carried towards the burning area. There is no easy solution here except to get out before the flames take a serious hold. Liferafts and flames are not good companions and flames will always win.

It is good to see that most modern powerboats and even some sailboats have a built-in fire extinguishing system for the engine compartment. This means that the system need only be triggered, usually from the helm, but the air intakes must be closed for it to be fully effective. The system will only work once. There is no second chance if the fire is not extinguished at the first attempt. Do not be tempted to open up the engine hatches too early to see if the fire is out or it may be given the new feed of oxygen that it is looking for. That time would be much better spent calling for help on the radio before the fire possibly puts the electrical system and the radio out of action.

While steel yachts offer a degree of safety in a fire, fibreglass boats do not, as the fibreglass itself will burn. It is possible to produce a fibreglass laminate that is fire resistant, but the added chemicals reduce the strength of the laminate, so it is generally not used for boat hulls and superstructures. Photographs of fibreglass boats burning show how the boat will burn from end to end.

Marina fires

Fires in marinas and boatyards account for the destruction of many yachts and while not exactly disasters at sea, they can still be dramatic because of the number of vessels involved. In 2002, close to 30 boats were destroyed in a boatyard fire in the United States. This demonstrates the combustibility of fibreglass boats and the high risk of fire spreading.

The yacht *Strumpet* caught fire when a Camping Gaz light fell off a hook and the still-hot glass ignited a fire in a sleeping bag, followed by a foam mattress, the wood lining of the cabin and finally the fibreglass of the hull. Fortunately, another yacht was close enough to rescue the crew because the inflatable dinghy on the coachroof had caught fire and melted. The entire yacht burned down to the waterline and sank. The owner thought that it was just 15 minutes from the first smell of smoke to the boat becoming a raging inferno.

A fire on a motor yacht in Brighton Marina is thought to have been caused by a gas leak that in turn triggered an explosion when the gas caught fire. The boat was destroyed, and set fire to only one neighbouring boat, as marina staff managed to move most of the adjacent boats away from the blaze. The one person who was on board the yacht when the blaze began escaped with burns that were serious enough for him to be hospitalised.

A more serious gas explosion occurred in Poole Harbour in 1999 when leaking gas in the bilges of the Joint Services sailing yacht *Lord Trenchard* exploded when triggered by a spark from the generator. The strength of the gas blast was such that the explosion was heard four miles away and windows on the adjacent quay were shattered. The boat was nearly destroyed, with the cockpit and coachroof blown away and the hull split. Two of the crew had just gone ashore and of the two remaining on board, one lost a leg. It was incredible that no one was killed. If this accident had occurred at sea with the full crew on board, the consequences could have been catastrophic. Investigation into the accident suggested that a leaking gas connection combined with a leaking gas locker had allowed gas to build up in the bilges. The gas alarm wasn't operating, and the

Fires in confined spaces can be very dangerous to other vessels.

generator spark triggered the explosion. Gas on boats works well if the systems are well-maintained and regularly checked, but it does not take much to turn a supposedly safe system into disaster.

When a vessel has a fire in harbour, or in the approaches to harbour, the situation can escalate quickly. Take the case of two tugs that were assisting a container ship into a berth. It was fortunate that the ship was partially secured to the berth when a fire started on one of the tugs. The tug engine had to be stopped to fight the fire and the second tug took it into a berth where the fire could be tackled from the shore. This was a relatively happy outcome, but any engine or steering failure in harbour is likely to have serious consequences. A fire in the engine compartment means the engine must be stopped, otherwise it is still sucking in fresh air that will feed the fire. Ships, like many small craft, have a gas-injection system to smother a fire in the engine compartment. Before the gas can be injected into the engine compartment, all air vents must be closed and the engine (or engines), stopped. The fire-quelling gas will not be able to replace oxygen in the compartment with inert gas if air vents are open or if the engines are running and sucking in more air.

This is a great system, as long as there is room for the vessel to drift while fighting the fire. That is rarely the case in harbour, so one disaster can lead to another, particularly when big ships are involved. Engine fires on ships manoeuvring in harbour present a serious risk when the ships carry dangerous cargoes such as liquid gas. Having two engines does not solve the problem, as they will both be housed in the same compartment.

Fire extinguishers

Most modern powerboats have engine fire systems installed, but sailboats with small engines must rely on fire extinguishers to do the job. I am always concerned about fire extinguishers on boats, largely because canisters small enough to handle on a boat moving around at sea are rarely adequate to tackle anything but the smallest fire. A larger canister requires two hands to hold and operate, leaving the operator without a hand to steady himself and the aim of the jet. One does not often hear of fires in their early stages tackled successfully on a yacht and most reports suggest that they get out of hand very quickly. It is time to think about better fire detection systems on small craft, in the accommodation as well as in the machinery spaces. As for fighting the fire, there is nothing as good as the water that surrounds the boat, but means are needed to get it from the sea to the seat of the fire. High voltages from a generator must be turned off before water can be used to quell a fire. It is a complex situation and one where it is not easy to find a satisfactory solution; when you have a fire at sea, panic is never very far away.

Small boat fires create enough drama for the crew, but it is the really big fires that are most dramatic of all. These tend to occur on passenger ships, which should have the best fire prevention systems available, but often seem not to. Scrutiny of the records show, that fires on passenger ships occur with monotonous regularity, at the rate of around five per year. While lessons are learned, the rules governing fire prevention and equipment never seem to quite catch up. This is probably because the rules are written to tackle most logical fire scenarios, but fail to take into account human behaviour, and it is impossible to draft rules that will cover every human error.

Throughout history there have been many fires in passenger ships; the case of the SS *Amazon* back in the 1850s is a good example. The death toll in modern ship fires is not so high, but fires still occur. The liner *Achille Lauro* has to be one of the world's unluckiest ships, suffering major fires in 1965 and 1972. Subsequently, three people were killed in a fire in one of the bars on board in 1981. *Achille Lauro* will be best remembered for being the subject of a hijack in 1985, but it was in 1994 that the ship was finally lost to a major fire that started in the engine room when off the African Coast. The crew fought the fire but it spread rapidly. Eventually the captain ordered 'Abandon ship' and nearly 1,000 passengers were rescued by passing ships, but two deaths and eight injuries resulted. The *Achille Lauro* burnt from end to end, and finally sank when under tow two days later.

Passenger ships

The same year the cross-Channel passenger ship *Sally Star* suffered an engine room fire caused, as many ship's fires are, by leaking fuel meeting a hot surface. The crew managed to extinguish the fire with the on-board equipment. The passengers were evacuated and the ship was towed into Dunkirk for repairs. On this occasion most of the ship's systems seemed to work – there is always a very fine line between success and failure.

One of the worst passenger ship disasters in recent years occurred when fire swept through the ferry, *Scandinavian Star*, while enroute between Norway and Denmark. The fire was thought to have been started by an arsonist and 159 people lost their lives. *Scandinavian Star* had been a cruise ship in a previous life, but the enquiry into the fire found that the ship's lifeboats were rotted or missing and insufficient fire alarms had been fitted. Since that time I have found reports of 18 fires on cruise ships, the latest being the *Calypso,* which had to be towed into Southampton after a fire started when the ship was in the English Channel. Fortunately, no one was hurt in this blaze and the subsequent investigation found the cause of the fire was a failed low-pressure fuel pipe. Apparently this failure had been noted as a problem on the engines fitted to *Calypso,* and although the manufacturers had recommended modifications, they had never been carried out.

Even the largest cruise ships are not immune from fire. In 2006 the *Star Princess* was on a passage from Grand Cayman in the Bahamas to Jamaica when a fire started on one of the stateroom external balconies. The fire spread rapidly to adjacent balconies and staterooms, resulting in one passenger death. The external balconies were not covered by the same strict requirements for fire-retardant materials as the interior of the ship. In a remarkably quick response, these rules have now been changed.

The *Star Princess* had over 3,800 people on board, but cruise ships are ever increasing in size, with the latest ships carrying around 5,000 people. There is growing recognition that it would be virtually impossible to evacuate this number quickly and safely. This has resulted in a change in safety emphasis: the ship is now considered to be the safest place in the event of a fire. Steps have been taken in ship design and equipment to ensure that there will always be safe areas on board in case of a fire. It sounds like an interesting alternative, but does this mean that in the future ships will no longer need to carry lifeboats and liferafts?

It was thought that the passenger ferry **Al Salam Boccaccio** *caught fire because the passengers were cooking meals on the car deck. She later capsized with a huge loss of life.*

The fire on the cruise liner Star Princess started on one of the cabin balconies and quickly spread. The fire regulations did not cover these outside areas of the ship.

The *Wind Song,* a sailing cruise ship, caught fire off Tahiti in 2002. Once again, the cause was an engine room fire and despite reports suggesting it was 'purely accidental', several explosions were heard after the fire broke out. All the passengers and most of the crew were evacuated in the ship's lifeboats and were picked up by a passing ship. Some crew remained on board to continue fighting the fire and the ship was eventually towed to port. There were no injuries or deaths in this incident, but a friend who was on board at the time described the events as traumatic.

The worst passenger ship disaster in recent years, and one of the worst-ever disasters at sea, was the sinking of the ferry *Al Salam Boccaccio 98.* This Ro-Ro ferry was running its regular route across the Red Sea, from Saudi Arabia to Egypt, when it is reported to have first caught fire, then capsized and sank. Over 1,000 lives were lost in this night-time disaster and, at the time of writing, a full report into the causes has yet to be published. However, the likely circumstance is that the disaster began with a fire on the car deck, where some passengers were cooking their evening meal. That in itself shows a very casual attitude to safety, but when the crew tackled the blaze with fire hoses they introduced water onto the car deck, and from that time the ship was on the downhill path to disaster. The water on the car deck could not drain away because the drains were blocked with debris. This led to a build-up of water on the car deck, which created a large free surface water effect similar to that found on the *Herald of Free Enterprise.* This resulted in a list, but it was when the ship apparently turned around to head back to its departure port that the water on the car deck created a surge to one side. That surge, coupled with the list generated by the ship turning, caused the vessel to capsize.

If these events did take place as described, it demonstrates once again how easy it is for one minor problem to escalate to the point of disaster. If rules and regulations had banned people from the car deck while at sea, as happens on most Ro-Ro ferries, that initial fire would have been prevented. At worst the vessel may have been stopped and required a tow to harbour but the passengers would have been safe. If the car deck drains had not been blocked, the situation would not have escalated as it did. These two human errors brought the safety levels down to zero. If the proposal to make areas of the ship a place of refuge for passengers had been enacted, then they might have been safe in the short term. In the long-term, however, they would have been far from safe. The reports suggest there wasn't time to escape in the lifeboats when the ship capsized, and this was a sequence of events that it was becoming increasingly difficult to recover from. Introducing water onto the car deck to quell a fire, blocked drains, a failure to appreciate the seriousness of the situation and apparently no distress message for help were all contributory factors.

A sequence of events

It is rare that one single event causes a disaster. A disaster is much more likely to be the result of a sequence of events occurring one after the other in a situation that becomes more complex as it deteriorates. The safety rules, as currently written, only review individual failures, such as an engine room fire or having the means to fight a fire or evacuate the ship. The rules ensure vessels have the means to cope with these individual events, but do not make allowances for safety equipment failing to work, two failures occurring simultaneously or, perhaps more pertinently, human failures that occur when coping with disaster.

The effort to prevent escalating failures is currently focused on passenger shipping, where the ships are becoming ever more complex and integrated. However, this problem applies to all vessels. Fire at sea is often the initial cause of a disaster, as it seems to have been the *Al Salam*, but this could just as easily have happened on a small yacht. Take the case where we rescued the owner from his burning boat. Who would have thought that a steering gear failure could have resulted in a fire? The question is: how do we find a solution to this compounding safety problem? It is quite easy to find a solution to individual events, but the problems start when that initial response does not work. Throughout this book, there will be cases where situations have started from very little, but have quickly escalated into total disaster.

The current solution is to have all the recommended safety equipment on board – perhaps even more than required levels. It is vital to know and understand how to use it effectively, because the best equipment in the world is useless unless operated correctly. Good maintenance is essential on both the safety equipment and all the mechanical and electrical systems on board. I find it hard to envisage a world where fires at sea are eliminated, but try not to let them happen to you. There is a need to recognise the potential seriousness of a situation. Finally, in the event of any disaster at sea, calling for help should be one of the first actions you take.

The increase in terrorist activity has added a whole new factor to the fire safety considerations of passenger ships. The *Achille Lauro* was hijacked in 1985, but the modern terrorist risk has increased the possibility of bombs on board. Probably most at risk from this threat are the Ro-Ro passenger ferries where little is done to check the contents of vehicles entering the car decks. It has been reported that the police foiled a terrorist plot to place a van containing explosives on board the ferry *Pont Aven* that sails between Santander and Plymouth. The car deck of a ferry appears to be the perfect location for a vehicle bomb, and it seems inevitable that in the future we will see closer monitoring of the vehicles. There are already enough problems with passenger shipping and fires, but when you factor in the risk of bombs on board, life on board passenger shipping may never be the same again.

MARINE ACCIDENT INVESTIGATION BRANCH

Fire: put it out and keep it out

Narrative

The owner and his wife were halfway through a four week holiday, cruising the Western Isles of Scotland, when fire gutted their 25m steel hulled yacht, forcing them to abandon ship. Fortunately no one was hurt, but the yacht was burnt out.

The yacht was on a daytime passage between two ports. On sailing, the weather had been clear, but around midday the wind had dropped and visibility reduced to less than 1 mile, so they were motor-sailing. About 1½ hours later, the crew noticed smoke coming up the companionway, and the skipper went to investigate. On lifting the companionway steps, the skipper saw flames on the starboard side of the engine in the vicinity of the wiring loom. He fetched a fire extinguisher from the forepeak and with 3–4 blasts put the fire out. The engine had remained running throughout.

There was a lot of smoke below, so the skipper went on deck for some fresh air before inspecting the damage. While on deck, he noticed that the instruments were no longer working, so assumed the fire had damaged the cables. He decided not to dampen down the fire area or stop the engine as he might have trouble restarting it, and there was insufficient wind to sail out of any trouble. However, he was unable to commence repairs due to residual smoke in the engine space, so he left the hatches open to try to clear it.

Fifteen minutes later, the skipper had gone below and forward to collect tools to begin repairs when he heard a shout from his wife, alerting him to black smoke emitting from the engine space and the wet locker area. As he left the cabin, he saw flames coming from the vicinity of the wet locker, and within minutes of his arriving in the cockpit, flames were rising through the companionway. At that point, the skipper decided to abandon ship and he and his wife, both wearing lifejackets, inflated and boarded their dinghy safely. Without a portable VHF in the liferaft, the skipper alerted the coastguard using his mobile phone.

The skipper and his wife were rescued by a nearby motorboat, and the local RNLI lifeboat fought the fire before taking the yacht in tow. Unfortunately, the extent of damage below was so great that it was not possible to determine the exact cause of the original fire, nor whether the second fire was a reignition of the first, or another fire caused by heat transfer into the wet locker.

The Lessons

Never assume a fire is out. To burn, a fire needs 3 ingredients: combustible material, oxygen and a source of ignition. Depriving the fire of any of these will put it out, temporarily. Firefighting must always be followed by action to permanently deprive the fire scene of at least one of the 3 key ingredients.

If you do suffer a fire on board, always check adjacent compartments and spaces for hot spots and secondary fires. If possible, dampen down hot spots, but at least monitor the area until any residual heat has dissipated.

Review your firefighting appliances

- Have you enough?
- Are they the right type?
- Are they in date?
- Are they positioned sensibly?
- Do you and your crew know how to use them?

Finally, review and if possible practise your 'abandon ship' drill. Check you know the contents of the liferaft and, if necessary, use a grab bag to hold supplementary kit such as a hand-held VHF and GPS.

With our modern navigation aids it would seem impossible to go aground but this large container ship managed it in spectacular fashion on the Greek coast.

Grounding

Nothing can prepare you for the shock of grounding. It is a cataclysmic event that would certainly never be part of your navigation plan. When your boat hits the rocks your world is suddenly transformed; it is not just the shock of the unexpected, but also the feeling of guilt. This is the moment when you know that you have made expensive navigational errors and there is not likely to be any turning back. Going aground will, at the least, destroy your self-confidence as a navigator, but it could equally destroy your professional career. Historically ships went aground because they might have been blown ashore at the mercy of the elements as often as a navigating mistake was made. These days there is little or no excuse and the blame can be laid fairly and squarely on the navigator's doorstep.

GPS

In theory it shouldn't be possible to run aground in the modern world. If your GPS is working (and even if it isn't you should have a portable backup), then you know where you are to an accuracy of 20–30m. This needs qualifying, because the GPS only gives a position in latitude and longitude and these are meaningless figures unless you can plot them on a chart. Once you can see your position on the chart in relation to the land and other dangers, you should be able to keep your vessel in deep water and avoid running aground. With the latest in modern electronic chart systems it is even possible for the equipment to sound a warning if you approach dangerous rocks or shallows.

You can't get a more embarrassing situation than this. The vessel has run aground right under the lighthouse.

Before electronics

It sounds so simple. So why do ships and boats continue to run aground? Back in the 1950s when I first went to sea, we had some excuse for running aground. When the ship was out of sight of land, any position was fixed by taking sights, using the sextant and the chronometer. If we were lucky that position might be accurate to within a mile, which was accurate enough in the open ocean. When land was in sight, the position was fixed with compass bearings and soundings and any such position might be accurate to within a few hundred feet. These position fixes were precise enough for most navigation requirements, and we would build in safety margins to make allowances for any inaccuracies, so most of the time we kept out of trouble. I think the fact that we had to coax the information out of the available data gave us a more accurate and reliable sense of position and we navigated accordingly.

The real problems came when we were making a landfall and the skies had been overcast for two or three days beforehand. You cannot get a position fix with a sextant when it is overcast so we had to rely on dead reckoning, working out where we should be by applying the course and speed of the ship to the plot and making allowances for the effects of winds, tides and currents. Dead reckoning was a bit like intelligent guesswork: most of the time it succeeded and land was sighted or soundings found before we got into serious trouble. Our approach was always cautious because we could never be quite sure where we were. The tides were one of the major areas of guesswork, particularly as they can get stronger near the land and have a considerable effect on the course made good of a 10 knot ship. Winds, when they were on the beam, could also generate a considerable amount of leeway which also had to be estimated. In clear weather we hoped to see the dangers before we hit them, but in fog our only guides were the fog signals and the soundings. It could become really scary, and there were times when we had to wait for the fog to clear before making a landfall.

The crew lay out an anchor to hold this yacht in position when the tide rises and to prevent it being swept further into the shallow water.

Electronic position-fixing systems such as Decca Navigator and Loran started to change all that. These systems were still prone to fixed and variable errors so the accuracy was not as good as we might have liked, but it took some of the guesswork out of position fixing. It was GPS that made all the difference. Here was a reliable source of accurate positions day and night, in good or bad visibility and with a degree of accuracy that would have been the envy of early navigators. Now there were no excuses for getting it wrong. I think it is the very ease of being able to fix positions accurately that could be responsible for vessels still going aground today.

Navigation

When the navigator had to coax positions out of very little information, sometimes struggling to get a fix or at least a position line, the navigator concentrated on navigation. Studying the chart intently, the navigator would focus on all the options available because they were fixing the position in relation to the land, so the relationship between safe waters and danger was clear to see. Today the position is plotted automatically on the electronic chart with a high degree of accuracy and there is a line marked on the chart for the route you want to follow. It is so easy – just keep the plot of the position on or close to the course line you want to follow and everything should be OK.

The trouble is that the ease and apparent accuracy of navigation means that things get taken for granted, safety margins get cut and checks aren't carried out. With GPS plotting it can look perfectly safe to have a narrow margin of safety when passing close to rocks or shoals, but that margin may be too small if things go wrong. You might not have detected a set of the tide towards the shoal, or the leeway may be more than expected and you didn't notice the set away from the plotted track. Worse still, a power or steering failure could leave no margin in which to drift, or to get the anchor down before the vessel grounds.

Take the case of the container ship *Alva Star*. The navigator on watch made an error when navigating at night off the Greek coast and hit the cliffs full tilt, ending up hard aground with the bow buried in the rocks. The radar should have shown up the danger and soundings would have given warning, but still she went aground. Another container ship, the *Anja*, did much the same thing on the rocky coast of Norway and it was three days before they managed to get her refloated.

This charter boat has run aground near the shore and been holed so it flooded when the tide rose.

This motor cruiser ran aground at speed onto the rocks off Norway.

The human factor

With all the positive preciseness of modern navigation there is still the human factor, which brings a large unknown into the navigation equation. If something like a quarter of all collisions at sea occur without one or more of the watchkeepers even being aware of the other ship before they hit, then the same can happen when ships go aground. You may wonder how a watchkeeper can be unaware of an approaching ship or cliffs, but think about it. Think about having just one person on the bridge, think about falling asleep, think about having too much to drink, think about fatigue and illness or even talking on a mobile phone. All of these things happen, and in modern navigation, on both ships and yachts, we still rely heavily on human intervention to make the correct decisions. If a fully equipped cruise liner can run aground on the Nantucket Shoals because the navigating officer didn't realise that the GPS was giving him dead reckoning information rather than a true position because the antenna was disconnected, then it is not too difficult to see how similar mistakes can be made on less well-manned ships and boats. One of the reasons cited for the large number of ship collisions and groundings is that the navigator on watch is making important decisions on his own without monitoring or verification. This means that mistakes do not get picked up at an early stage and can lead to disaster.

The Malaysian container ship *Bunga Teratai Satu* was travelling through the passage inside the barrier reef off the Australian coast, and had just dropped its pilot (who had controlled the vessel through the narrow part of the passage). The course was set to the next waypoint, where a significant alteration of course was required but not initiated. The ship carried on and struck a reef while travelling at 20 knots. The reason that no action was taken was that the officer on watch was busy talking on his mobile phone to his family while the ship was still within range of shore

This sailing yacht is high and dry on the rocks after making a navigation error.

reception. It could be that there was an added distraction because the officer's wife was also on the bridge at the time. The officer was lucky and no damage was done to the ship, but the coral reef suffered considerably. It could also have been distraction of the officer on watch that caused the *Kowloon Bay*, a large container ship, to hit a rock off the coast of Indonesia when travelling at 21 knots. The grounding was at night and there was no light on the rock, but it was certainly big enough to make a significant radar target, so there is no real excuse.

The grounding of the *Sealand Express* is more understandable: she was at anchor in strong winds and the anchor dragged. In the big seas that were running at the time the ship was blown onto the beach, and became the subject of a major salvage operation.

It happens to yachts

Yachts can do the same thing and there is a tale of a yachtsman who left his girlfriend on watch while he went below; during his quick nap she managed to run the boat aground. That does not sound like a good basis for a happy relationship! There are many yachts that seem to have a similar casual attitude to navigation and trouble starts when the person on watch is distracted by his mobile phone or some sort of domestic emergency. Navigation seems so easy these days that there is no longer the same focus on what is happening, and it is so easy to forget to make a course alteration at the right moment when running under autopilot, or even to look forward to see what lies ahead. There will almost always be some visual clue about dangers before you hit them. When the cruise liner went aground on the Nantucket Shoals, the lookout reported white water ahead some time before she grounded.

This ship ran aground and stayed there for three days on the wintery coast of Norway.

Keeping your eyes open

I relied heavily on visual clues when we were navigating across the Nantucket Shoals at 50 knots in *Virgin Atlantic Challenger II*. We were taking the shortest possible route across the Atlantic in order to set a new record, and I chose a course across the shoals rather than go round them as it would save us two hours. It was a calculated risk, but I reasoned that I would see any waves that might damage us breaking on shallow water, and so focused on the view ahead with Loran giving us position information. It was just as well I did, because I found out later that there had been no up-to-date surveys of the area as no one went there.

The Nantucket Shoals have been a graveyard for ships over the years, with many notable disasters taking place over these extensive shallows. The *Argo Merchant* was one of the first of the major oil pollution disasters when she grounded on the shoals in 1976 and spilled 7.6 million gallons of oil. Luckily the wind was blowing offshore so the pollution effects were limited. Even the liner *Queen Elizabeth II* was not immune and she touched bottom in shallow water in 1992 when passing through Vineyard Sound at 25 knots, damaging the hull bottom and the propellers.

Drifting ashore

There can be even more dramatic events when ships and boats drift ashore. Car carriers are huge ships specifically designed for carrying thousands of cars. They are very high-sided and in the event of an engine failure will drift rapidly. That was why urgent action was needed when the car carrier *Figaro* lost power when passing through the shipping lanes between Land's End and the Scilly Isles off the south-west point of Britain. In a couple of hours she would have been close to the rocks. A coastguard tug took her in tow, only to have the tow line part in gale-force winds and big seas. Finally the ship got her engine started again and made it to harbour.

The ship lost power because the engine room fire-extinguishing system was set off accidentally and that automatically shut down the engine. Many modern engines with electronic controls will shut down automatically under certain circumstances, and this is a considerable worry because the shutdown does not take into account the ship's situation. Two engines would still be in the same compartment, so they would still both shut down. The blame for this situation should not be placed on the ship's crew, but on the basic design fault that allows a ship to become helpless when the engine shuts down automatically. It seems that the engineers who design the engine systems are only concerned with the fate of the engine, and not the fate of the ship. Virtually all powerboats now have electronically controlled engines and my concern is that they take too much control out of the hands of the crew. There are few choices when the engine shuts down automatically; you can only make the best of a bad job.

A gas carrier running aground is a nightmare scenario, but exactly that happened recently on the coast of the Dominican Republic. Fortunately the 551ft SCF *Tomsk* had part-discharged her cargo, but there were still 1.5 million gallons of liquefied petroleum gas on board when she was hit by a tropical storm. This parted the moorings and she blew ashore but the double hull structure prevented pollution and leaks.

This is not to say that grounding never happened in the old days. I ran aground on my first trip to sea in 1947. I was in the Sea Scouts and somehow we got hold of a redundant naval launch and enough fuel to run down the Thames and around to Ramsgate. All went well until the approach to Ramsgate where our progress was brought to an abrupt halt as we ran aground on a sandbank. Even though I was a novice and not even navigating at that time, there was some excuse for the grounding: we were using pre-war charts. When the lifeboat pulled us off, the crew said that the sandbank we hit had built up during the war and was not even shown on the latest charts because there had been no time for surveys. Excuses may help the navigator's conscience but you have still run aground, which is never good news. As a navigator you are rather like a football goalkeeper: you tend to get remembered by the ones you get wrong, not the ones you get right.

*The bow damage to the **Alpha Action** was considerable after she ran aground on rocks.*

The problem with GPS

One of the problems that navigators face when presented with the wonderful accuracy of GPS is that it is anonymous. The position is just a latitude and longitude; numbers that bear no relation to the topography around you. The electronic chart helps to translate that position into something that you can recognise, and will show your position in relation to the rocks and shoals that you are trying to avoid, but when you had to take compass bearings to fix your position you had a much more intimate relationship with the dangers around you. The dangers became very real and you had an awareness that doesn't come from the bland presentation of the modern electronic chart.

In most cases grounding comes as a sudden and horrible shock. There was a case a few years back, where a 28ft sports cruiser was on passage from Salcombe to Plymouth and preparing to enter the harbour in the early hours of the morning. The navigation appeared to be in good hands, with an Admiralty pilot from Plymouth using his long years of experience to give the inexperienced owner a helping hand.

It is not quite clear what caused the boat to hit the vertical face of a rock at a speed of over 20 knots, but the result was pretty catastrophic. Hitting a vertical wall at 20 knots means the boat stops dead on impact, but the crew do not. The pilot was on the helm and probably got a couple of seconds' warning to brace himself against the impact. The owner was not so lucky; the lower half of his body was held against a rigid part of the cockpit and the top half was thrown forward so that his face smashed against the dashboard.

This German patrol boat was on a courtesy visit to Norway when it hit the rocks at speed and ended up high and dry.

The pilot swore the boat must have hit a floating container or similar wreckage, but a planing boat hitting that sort of object would tend to ride up over it and not stop quite so abruptly. There is no doubt that the pilot had made a mistake, perhaps with the lights on shore or other navigation marks, and mistook the position of the boat so that it ran full tilt into the rock. The position of the wreckage tends to corroborate this, although it did drift some way off before sinking. Luckily, help was at hand to rescue the occupants before the boat sank. Plotting the GPS positions on an electronic chart would have shown up the approaching danger in time to avoid it.

This ship was so close to the shore when it went aground that they could put the gangway out to walk ashore.

Very sudden stops

Colliding with a vertical rock face is likely to be one of the most sudden stops that a vessel will experience, and injury to the crew is highly probable as they will be thrown about. However, even with a vertical rock face there is likely to be underwater shoaling that the ship will hit before it meets the rock and this should make the stop a bit more gradual and provide some sort of warning, but the shock will still be there.

Going into Singapore Harbour one night when I was a young apprentice at sea gave me my first experience of grounding in a ship. The ship's captain was drunk, a not uncommon experience in

The container ship APL Panama ran aground off Mexico when the captain tried to enter port without a pilot.

those days, and full of confidence in his ability to take the ship to an anchorage without the help of a pilot. With no warning, the ship touched bottom and heeled over under the impact but kept going. The captain must have known that he was running out of luck, and he dropped anchor as the ship was obviously not where he'd thought.

All of the tanks were sounded to see if there were any leaks but everything seemed to be holding tight, so we waited until daylight when divers could go down to inspect the bottom of the ship. The captain was very lucky because although the hull plating was bent in between the frames where it had hit the rocks, there was no penetration of the hull. In addition to this the bilge keel was bent and distorted. After discharging the cargo, we were given the go ahead to steam to Calcutta where the ship was scheduled to go into dry dock anyway, and could be checked out in detail.

One night on the passage to Calcutta, the engine room phoned the bridge: 'I can hear something banging on the outside of the hull.' Well, in theory, there couldn't be anything out there banging on the hull, but the sound got louder and louder until it could be heard throughout the ship. What on earth could it be? In less enlightened days it would be easy to imagine it as being a warning sign from the deep, but after a few hours the banging suddenly stopped. With no idea of what could have caused the noise we duly arrived in Calcutta and went into dry dock, and there the mystery was solved. We knew that the bilge keel had been bent and distorted in the grounding, and now two-thirds of it were missing altogether. The banging had been caused by the forward end of it waving around in the water, passing the hull, and then hitting the side of the hull.

Sudden stops at sea

Another case where a captain refused a pilot, and in this case tug assistance as well, was aboard the container ship APL *Panama*, when entering a port in Mexico. This was on Christmas Day in 2005 and no allowance was made for the strong currents and wind in the entrance, with the result that the ship was grounded near the port entrance.

I am not sure whether the following incident qualifies as a grounding or a collision, but what is certain in another case is that the captain was drunk when his 2,000 tonne ship collided with a gas platform in the North Sea and sank. However, the consequences could have been much more serious. I suppose it is inevitable when you park a collection of platforms and drilling rigs in the busy waters of the North Sea and the Gulf of Mexico that sometime, somewhere a ship is going to collide with one of them. The platforms are a blaze of light at night and they have a 500m exclusion zone set up around them as well as a standby ship patrolling, so the area should be safe. However, if a ship is on a course for collision and the watchkeeper is drunk, asleep or otherwise incapable, then none of these safety measures are going to stop it. The crew were rescued by the

This brand new motor cruiser hit the rocks on its maiden voyage in Norway.

platform's stand-by vessel before the ship sank and fortunately the damage to the gas rig was minimal, but even so the cost of the accident was huge as production had to be stopped until the platform could be checked.

An incident of this type involving a large tanker and an oil platform could turn into a major human disaster, as well as an environmental one. There is no easy way of preventing such an accident, short of having a large tug at each installation with the capability of diverting a ship away. A workboat operating in the Gulf of Mexico had a similar experience when the vessel struck a wellhead. Several of the crew were injured, but there were no fatalities in what must have been a very sudden stop.

The importance of engines

Modern ships have the power and capability to keep away from land, but the sailing ships of old had a dread of becoming embayed on a lee shore, and being unable to tack their way off must have been a nightmare. Those square-rigged sailing ships would be lucky to sail at an angle of anything less than 60 degrees off the wind. Even when they tried to sail at this angle to escape from a lee shore, the leeway that the ship would make meant that they could not make a course over the ground of much less than 90 degrees off the wind. With land sticking out at each end of the bay there was little hope of getting off once they were trapped inside the bay in a strong wind. Anchoring was the only possible solution, but it was asking a lot for an anchor to hold in those conditions. Modern sailboats can sail much closer to the wind, probably up to 45 degrees, but that risk of a lee shore still remains, although of course modern boats also have engines to help.

It is not so much that yachts do not have the capability to sail away from the land when the wind is onshore, but in a strong blow the sails they will be using will be reefed down or shortened and less efficient, so the yacht will not sail as close to the wind as it might need. Ground will also be lost every time that the yacht tacks and the crew may be tired and slow, so there still is a risk of being blown onshore. A powerful engine can be the key to getting out of this sort of trouble but, better still, a good safety margin offshore can prevent it in the first place.

Leeway

Leeway can be the big unknown factor in navigation as there is no reliable way to measure it, particularly in strong winds. With modern GPS it is possible to detect the leeway as it happens, by watching the position of the vessel as it drifts away from the required course line on the chart. Sailboats have to put up with leeway as a fact of life when they are tacking into the wind or with the wind on the beam, and most skippers will know what to expect from experience. The speed of

A fast sports cruiser rescued after going aground on rocks.

The underwater damage caused through grounding of this fast sports cruiser, with severe damage to the hull and the propellers torn off.

advance of a fast boat will make the leeway almost insignificant, although steering bias where the helmsman steers a course away from the wind as a sort of instinctive reaction can become a form of leeway. Leeway can also be quite a problem on ships running without cargo. It was the leeway generated in a storm on the west coast of Scotland that caused the most serious grounding in my long career.

I had been transferred to the 6,000 tonne ship *Tapti* on a temporary basis, for a trip around the north of Scotland from Liverpool to the Tyne. The *Tapti* had discharged her cargo in Liverpool and was heading round to the east coast to start loading the next cargo. It was in the depths of winter, when the gales come rolling in from the Atlantic, and this trip held the promise of some very uncomfortable conditions until we rounded the top of Scotland and gained some shelter from the land on the east side.

Our planned route was up through the North Channel between Ireland and Scotland and then through the wide channel between the mainland and the Outer Hebrides. As a young apprentice I did not have any say in the navigation, but on this voyage I was keeping watch with one of the officers to gain experience. This time I got more experience than I bargained for.

The promised gale from the west materialised as we headed north, and by nightfall it was not only blowing violently but snowing hard as well, so we were in the teeth of a wild blizzard. The visibility was not much above zero in the swirling snow, and we were heading north virtually blind. The Minches Channel between mainland Scotland and the outer islands is quite wide and we had

This fishing boat went aground on rocks in Alaska and knocked down the beacon marking the rocks in the process.

got a good fix at the south end. Now under the shelter of the land at last, the sea conditions had become more comfortable, but for navigation we were relying entirely on dead reckoning, hoping that when the snow stopped we could pick up one of the many lights on the islands to get a fix. With the wind on the beam the ship was making a lot of leeway but the question was how much? With the ship running light, with no cargo on board, she was in fact going as much sideways as forwards.

We found out later just how much she was going sideways when, with a sickening grinding crunch, we hit the rocks. This was something of a gradual grounding, the ship ploughing up onto the rocky shore with the horrible sound of the bottom of the ship being torn out. The noise seems to go on for ever and it is one of the worst things you will ever hear in your life. Somehow I knew that the ship was not going to come off those rocks again and there was a feeling of finality to the situation. Even though the engine was put astern to try to get off the shore, the rocks had a firm hold. We seemed to be relatively safe where we were, although the waves were pounding the hull and sending spray over the decks. The ship was not going to sink where it lay, but we did not want to hang around in the blinding snow so a Mayday was sent out over the radio.

This was where the problems started. Because we didn't know where we were, we couldn't give an accurate position. However, radio stations on shore were able to take bearings of our radio transmissions and get a rough fix, and the lifeboat from Mallaig was called to our aid. The lifeboat was navigating virtually blind among the rocks and islands along that inhospitable coast, just as we had done, but by dawn the snow had relented and they found us impaled on the rocks between the islands of Rhum and Eigg. In what turned out to be quite a dramatic rescue, they took the whole crew off and we were landed in Tobermory to make the long trip home.

Now in theory, if we had had a GPS we would have known exactly where we were and that grounding would not have happened. However, I am not so sure; in that blizzard, the GPS antenna might have iced up, and ice on an antenna means that it cannot receive signals. I found this out on a trip along the east coast of America in winter, when the temperatures were well below zero and both the GPS and the radar stopped working because the spray was freezing on the antenna.

Local knowledge

Leeway can still be the curse of big modern ships, in spite of all their sophisticated navigation equipment. One of the high-sided cross-Channel passenger ships went aground near the entrance to Calais a few years ago because of leeway. The busy entrance channel there runs along parallel to the shore for the last few miles, and ships entering must keep to the starboard side, which is also the landward side. With a strong northerly wind blowing, this ship got too close to the edge of the channel after having to alter course to avoid some of the outward bound ships, and found that it was unable to steer clear. When trying to alter course to port to bring the ship away from the shallow water, the stern tends to swing in closer to the shallows, and there comes a point when going aground is inevitable, particularly with the wind still blowing the ship bodily sideways.

This ship must have made the same passage hundreds of times and this grounding sounds like a case of familiarity leading to a slightly casual approach. This has been the cause of many groundings and local knowledge can be both a good and a dangerous thing. Upon entering an unfamiliar harbour we have all heard a member of the crew say, 'I know this harbour. I've been here before', so you listen to their advice. When it turns out that they don't really know the harbour well at all, it can be too late.

I went aground in the Menai Straits because of this so-called local knowledge. The Menai Straits present a considerable navigation challenge at the best of times, but we were travelling through the twisting narrow channels as part of a race and so taking more chances than we ought. With the strong tide flowing with us there was no stopping or second chances, and at one of the markers there was no clear indication of which side to pass. 'Local knowledge' told us to leave it to port and the next thing we knew we hit a rock. It was a fairly gentle collision, more of a sliding onto the rock, and no damage was done, but we were quickly high and dry with the fast dropping tide and spent several uncomfortable hours leaning over at a steep angle until the tide rose again.

Problems for a keelboat

One of the problems with a sailboat grounding on a falling tide is that as the water drops away the boat can heel over at quite a steep angle because of the keel. A lot depends on the shape of the hull but few yachts will sit upright. Apart from being uncomfortable, this brings the risk of flooding as the tide rises because the water might enter the hull before the boat starts to float. If you should have the misfortune of going aground then try to make sure the hull leans away from the wind and waves as it dries out, and try to seal off the cabin companionway. Refloating is always an anxious moment, and having an anchor out can help to hold the boat while the tide rises, helping you to float clear.

Powerboat damage

Powerboats have a very different problem when they go aground. There is every chance that their rudders and propellers will be damaged, meaning that they have no astern power to get off. Going aground could also create a hole in the hull around the stern gland or the P-bracket attachments. The Fowey lifeboat was called out a few years ago to a beautiful wooden Riva that had hit the rocks just outside the entrance; fortunately they were quick enough to get hold of the boat, secure it alongside and get it to the boatyard before it sank. The grounding had ripped out its stern gear and the boat was on the verge of sinking.

The same thing happened with a brand new motor yacht in Norway. This 60-footer had just been launched and the proud owner was taking it out on its first run when he hit an isolated rock. The rudders and propellers were torn out of the stern, water poured in through the hole, and the boat sank. The worst part of that disaster was that the owner had not arranged his insurance before he sailed.

A powerboat grounding can be quite a spectacle, as a racing driver in Guernsey found out. There is a very high rise and fall of tide in the Channel Islands. This is not a problem for racing, but this driver made the mistake of not keeping to the channel when entering harbour after the race. He went aground at slow speed on a rock, not realising that this was an isolated pillar rock until the tide dropped, leaving the boat balancing, left high and dry. Going aground on the top of the tide can leave ships and boats high and dry in a dramatic isolation that advertises the mistake to everyone in sight.

Racing boats

Racing powerboats have had some spectacular accidents. One racer in Dubai lost control on a turn and carried straight on. His boat climbed a sloping breakwater wall and came to rest high and dry on the level ground at the top. Amazingly the crew escaped without a scratch, but it must have been a bumpy ride up that slope.

Racing driver Fabio Buzzi has claimed many world championships and records in his career, but one he would like to forget is the record for running aground at the highest speed! Fabio, who I have raced with for many years, was driving a single seater hydroplane in the Pavia to Venezia Race in Italy. This race goes down the River Po from Pavia and ends in Venice, and is open to any type of boat. Fabio had been trying to win the race for over 20 years and had had a couple of spectacular crashes in the process. The River Po twists and turns on its way down to the sea and there are extensive sand and mud banks to catch the unwary. To help with the navigation Fabio had the course that he wanted to follow entered on to a chart plotter, so that the GPS could do all the work of navigating and he simply had to keep the boat on the red line on the display.

The boat was one of the fastest that he has built, a 7m hydroplane, powered with a 1,000hp gas turbine. I have driven this boat on Lake Como and reached speeds of 150mph and that was not flat out, so I know it is seriously fast. Everything was set up for the big day, with Fabio driving the fastest boat in the race and using a navigation system that should allow him to avoid mistakes on the twisting river.

Everything was working well and Fabio was well ahead of the competition when the sun reflected off the angled chart display. He was now heading down the river virtually blind as there are

Fabio Buzzi ran aground at 150mph on the River Po in Italy after sun reflections meant that he could not read his navigation display.

no landmarks or buoyage to show where the channel is. Without being able to see the chart display, he missed the channel and hit a mud bank at over 150mph. That should have been the end of both boat and driver, but luck was on Fabio's side that day. The mud bank was both soft and perfectly contoured to allow the boat to cruise to a stop, high and dry but the right way up and in one piece.

The boat had carved its own channel through the soft mud and appeared to be undamaged so Fabio recruited 14 bystanders who were watching the race and persuaded them to pick up the boat and carry it back to the water. Climbing on board and firing up the turbine, he was back in the race. Unfortunately, however, the steering was bent, so he was forced to retire further downriver.

This cargo ship was left high and dry on the beach after the tide went out.

Is that land ahead?

Equally lucky were the crew of *Gentry Eagle*, the 110-footer that American Tom Gentry built to try to take the Atlantic record. On their first attempt at the record *Gentry* headed out into the Atlantic from New York, only to be forced back into St Johns, Newfoundland, by bad weather. We had left on the same day in *Azimut Atlantic Challenger* in a bid for the non-stop record across the Atlantic, but we were also forced out by an engine failure. We both ended up in Newfoundland, but *Gentry Eagle* got into trouble on her run back to New York.

Leaving St Johns with just a three-man crew, *Gentry Eagle* was heading down the coast of Nova Scotia in the dark using her radar for the navigation along the coast. John Connor was the skipper and the engineer was Eckie Rastig from MTU, who had been with us on *Virgin Atlantic Challenger*. The conversation is reported to have gone something like this:

Rastig:	'I think there is land ahead on the radar.'
Connor:	'That's not land, that's a thunderstorm.'
Rastig:	'I think its land.'
Connor:	'Nah, that's a thunderstorm.'

Cruising at over 40 knots, the next minute the boat hit the rocks on the shore at what must have been the highest grounding speed before Fabio took the record. It appears that when they hit the 'beach', comprised of huge boulders, the boat slid over them before coming to rest high and dry. The crew got ashore by climbing out through the bottom of the boat!

They were incredibly lucky. Once daylight came they could see that the 'beach' they hit was the only shelving piece of coast for miles around. On either side there were vertical cliffs that would have caused serious damage and injury. *Gentry Eagle* was salvaged and repaired and the next year she was out on the Atlantic again, on this occasion setting a record for the fastest-ever crossing achieved at that time.

Fast ferries

Going aground can have its humorous side, but it can also spell disaster. The new generation of fast ferries travel at speeds of over 40 knots, and present a considerable risk of injury and death to passengers if they go aground. If the ferry stops suddenly the passengers will keep going until they hit something solid. On most of the larger ferries, people can get up and walk around, which would increase the risk of injury in a grounding. You might think that grounding would be an unlikely event on these ferries, considering their professional crews, but it's not. A ferry in Norway hit the rocks at night after making a navigation mistake and this resulted in many injuries and some deaths. The grounding occurred when the ferry was rounding a rock that had a lighthouse on it. However, the flashing light was only on once every 30 seconds, and in the dark interval of the light, the ferry covered quite a distance, bringing it onto the rocks before the next flash. Familiarity with a route does tend to encourage navigators to cut corners and take the shortest route, but in this case the route was just a bit too short.

Another large wave-piercing fast ferry went aground when it was undergoing sea trials off the coast of Tasmania. The ferry had just been launched and it was doing the trials in familiar waters when it hit the rocks. There were no deaths or injuries, but these fast-ferry accidents do demonstrate how familiarity with local waters can encourage operators to reduce the safety margins and cut corners. When the margins are small it only needs a distraction or small mistake to lead to disaster.

Pollution

These days when it comes to shipping there seems to be more concern with the loss of oil than the loss of life. In virtually every major shipping disaster where a ship has run aground, the focus is now on the risk of oil pollution. I'd like to think that this is because the crew have been rescued at an early stage in the proceedings. There is no doubt that oil pollution is a serious matter, and there have been some major environmental disasters caused by carelessness or mechanical failure, but saving lives seems to have become almost a secondary consideration.

Pollution can occur close inshore if mistakes are made.

The names of the tankers that have caused serious pollution are embedded in maritime history. It started with the *Torrey Canyon*, when she hit the Seven Stones rocks off Land's End. Anti-pollution techniques were still in their infancy and the Air Force ended up bombing the wreck to try to set fire to the oil rather than let it leak out into the sea. Then there was the *Exxon Valdez* that went aground in Alaska; the *Amoco Cadiz* that hit the shores of Brittany in France and the *Sea Empress* that went ashore in the entrance to Milford Haven in Wales. Lately the *Braer* has hit

It can be embarrassing if this grounding happens in familiar waters.

the headlines in the Shetland Islands, and so it goes on. In spite of modern navigation systems and the latest technology on board, it does seem as though ship groundings are an inevitable part of the maritime scene, and the number of serious casualties show no sign of abating.

Now that most tankers are required to have double hulls, the risks of the cargo leaking are reduced, but tankers are still going aground. One of the latest occurred off New York when the 250m *White Sea* went aground through a navigation error. Fortunately the ship's oil tanks remained intact so there was no pollution, and after half the oil had been pumped out into another tanker, the ship was refloated. It is all too common an occurrence and I wonder why there is not more focus on prevention.

Engine failures

Mechanical failure seems to have taken over as the main cause of these groundings, so perhaps the introduction of GPS is having a positive effect on safety. However, it is hard to credit the wisdom of fitting these large and expensive ships, which have huge polluting potential, with a single engine and a single steering system. Even the yachtsman in his small powerboat can see the benefit of having two engines when he goes to sea. It does not take an Einstein IQ to realise that if you suffer engine failure at sea on a single-engine boat then you are at serious risk of losing your life or at least of losing your boat. When I first went to sea on a single-engine tramp ship, engine failures occurred with monotonous regularity. We were lucky that we had both the time and resources to fix things, but there were times when we spent a couple of days drifting on the ocean while the engineers rebuilt the engine. We were fortunate this didn't occur in bad weather or when we were close to land.

When the *Amoco Cadiz* went ashore off the French coast it was because of an engine failure. Perhaps engines have become more reliable on ships these days, but I can't help feeling that as designers try to squeeze more and more power out of less and less engine and fuel, the reliability may be taking something of a back seat. Certainly engines still stop or catch fire, and this may be a human or mechanical fault, but ships are still left drifting. I can't help feeling that the main reason given for so many ships running aground in harbours or their entrances is that there has been a steering or engine failure. Modern diesel engines have automatic shutdown systems that stop the engine automatically if the

Losing power and going aground near the entrance to a harbour.

monitoring system detects potential trouble. The navigators have no control over when the engine shuts down, and this must risk disaster if it happens at a critical navigation point.

I think it is very telling that the authorities in both France and the UK have established large tugs on station at critical points to cope with ships having mechanical failures. Hopefully the tugs will be able to connect a tow line before the ship drifts ashore. Once more this highlights the need for adequate safety margins to give time to solve the problem before the ship grounds. These tugs are a hugely expensive solution to a potential problem, but it was rather forced on the authorities as the only practical means of coping with the threat. We have heard the clamour for tankers to have double hulls to help reduce pollution, but I don't hear of any similar clamour to reduce the risks by insisting on two engines and two steering systems.

Backup systems

Even having two of everything does not prevent ships going ashore. The cruise liner *Sea Diamond* went aground, hitting rocks as it was anchoring off a harbour in Greece, simply though a navigation mistake. This was a major cruise ship with 1,500 passengers on board and everything was in the favour of the authorities to organise an orderly evacuation. But despite having 15 hours to evacuate the passengers and crew before the ship sank, two lives were lost. Cruise liners that will accommodate up to 5,000 passengers are now being built, which begs the question of how they might be evacuated in an emergency. It seems that the authorities are reluctant to address the problem because there is no obvious solution.

It could be argued that large cruise liners are so well organised and equipped that accidents on a major scale simply will not happen. But that was probably what was said about the *Sea Diamond*. How is it possible to legislate to prevent such disasters, except by putting a restriction on the size of ships operating in certain waters? There is so little international cooperation in setting standards that disasters like this will continue to happen.

Of course, mechanical failure is another possibility, but these ships should have enough of a backup system to prevent such a failure having any real impact. I have experienced the results of mechanical failure with no backup in narrow waters running up the Houston Ship Channel, when one of the crew accidentally turned the steam off the steering engine. There was no time to drop the anchor or reverse the engines before the ship veered into the shallows at the side of the channel. There was a similar case recently when a container ship was heading out to sea on the River Schelde in Belgium. This ship suffered a complete blackout of all the electrical systems on board. Every system on the ship relied on electrical power, so this failure stopped the engine and the steering, and the ship went aground.

Single engines

On the road a failure may leave you stranded, but not usually in danger. At sea you are in potential danger as soon as you lose control of engines, steering or sails, and probably also if you have an electrical failure. I find it hard to understand why backup systems are not insisted upon. These would allow you to get home under your own resources, rather than relying on someone else coming to your rescue before you hit the rocks. Governments have spent huge amounts of money on providing rescue tugs in sensitive coastline areas in the hope that they can get to a disabled vessel before it drifts ashore and starts polluting the shoreline. The same effort might be gainfully employed in providing some means of coping with the large numbers of passengers on cruise liners who could be at risk should the ship catch fire or go aground.

Fitting ships with single engines is done on the basis of economy. A single engine is both cheaper and more efficient than a twin installation, and even fast container ships use a single engine where possible. However, when you have two engines you not only have a backup in the event of one engine stopping, but you also have a backup steering system should the main one fail, because you can use two engines to steer the ship. It seems that the risks as a result of only having a single engine on ships, and on most fishing boats for that matter, are considered acceptable and governments and insurance companies are left to pick up the pieces when things go wrong.

Human error

In reality, human error is the primary cause of ships and boats grounding. It can be possible to find a solution for mechanical failures by insisting on higher standards, but finding a solution for human error is much more difficult. As we will see throughout this book it can be fatigue, drunkenness, or just plain inattention that is the primary cause of an accident. It is much harder to find a solution for these. History suggests that it will need a major disaster before any corrective action is taken.

MARINE ACCIDENT INVESTIGATION BRANCH

Secure anchorage proves to be anything but

Narrative

A 10.7m steel-hulled sailing yacht was being used for a five-day training course on the west coast of Scotland. Strong winds were being forecast for the coming night so it was decided to find a sheltered anchorage.

A bay was chosen that the skipper had used several times before and the yacht was anchored in 2.7m charted depth. A 16kg 'Delta' anchor was prepared with chain and warp, and a 7.5kg 'Bruce' type anchor was attached to the trip line eye of the 'Delta' with 4m length and a trip line and float attached. These were deployed as one unit, smaller first. This is a technique known as tandem anchoring. In addition, a 5kg 'angel' was rigged at

20m length of chain, and nylon warp increased the overall scope to 36m. The nature of the bottom was fine sand with some weed.

The anchors were set for a south west wind and were tested with the engine running astern while transits were observed. Everything appeared to be secure and the GPS alarm was set to 0.03 mile (about 55m). The barometer had been falling steadily all afternoon and, as the skipper and crew were turning in, was observed to be falling more rapidly. At this point the wind was observed to be south west force 6.

Just before midnight the GPS alarm woke the skipper. He jumped out of his berth and saw that they were 0.04 mile out of position. He started the engine and donned a lifejacket, telling his crew of four to do likewise. By the time he was on deck, the depth sounder was showing minimal depth, and almost immediately the keel touched the bottom. Attempts to motor off failed and the yacht soon listed by 20° to starboard, with the wind and sea on the port bow. A Pan Pan call was sent and acknowledged by the local coastguard. The local lifeboat was dispatched to the scene but had some distance to travel.

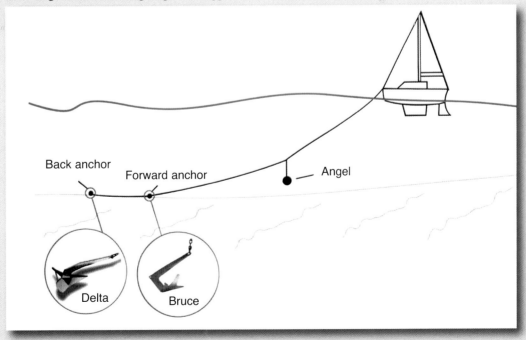

It was soon established that the yacht was on a reef and was being driven on by the weather. The angle of heel increased to 30°. The crew managed to recover the anchors during this time so that they could be deployed again when necessary.

By the time the lifeboat arrived, the skipper had established that the tide was on the rise and that the depth would soon be sufficient for them to float off. After more movement and pounding, they eventually came clear and were able to safely re-anchor. The yacht was lifted and inspected for damage, but was found to be unscathed.

The Lessons

1

On the night of the accident, a vigorous depression was passing across the north of the British Isles. The inshore waters forecast, issued by the Met Office at 1700, gave south force 5–7, increasing force 7–9, then veering west force 5–6. Weather records from the nearest weather station confirm that this forecast was accurate, with southerly wind speeds peaking between midnight and 0300 at force 7 with gusts of force 9. By 0400, the wind had veered west and had moderated. Setting the tandem anchors for a southwesterly made sense earlier in the afternoon when that wind direction was observed. However, the veering loads produced when the wind backed and freshened might have reduced the effectiveness of this anchoring arrangement.

2

However unappealing the setting of an anchor watch might be, a forecast giving high winds and changes of wind direction of 90° overnight might have given pause for thought in what was a relatively tight anchorage. GPS alarms are a useful aid, but in this case did not give the skipper enough time to react. Alarms have to be set to a range sufficient for them not to trigger every time the boat veers normally, but to sound when serious movement has taken place.

3

Tandem anchoring is a recognised technique for improving holding power on a single chain. However, there is a risk that when veering loads are applied, the forward anchor is at risk of rolling out of its set.

4

It was fortunate that the yacht grounded on a reef with safe water to leeward. If they had been driven onto a rocky lee shore, the outcome would most likely have been different.

This picture shows how much of an iceberg lies underwater, compared with the limited view that mariners get.

Ice

When the *Titanic* hit an iceberg in 1912 it was a defining moment in the history of safety at sea. Probably the most high profile event ever to take place on the Atlantic Ocean, it transformed the world of shipping and ship design. The sinking of a vessel hailed as 'unsinkable', which sailed without sufficient lifeboats for all its passengers and crew, focused attention on the vulnerability of shipping in general, and passenger ships in particular. It led to a new focus on lifesaving equipment, although some would still question whether this equipment is adequate for escape even today. It also concentrated attention on the structure of ships, but little has changed except that now, nobody claims that modern ships are unsinkable. In fact, as this book shows, boats and ships seem to be as vulnerable as ever.

Colliding with icebergs on the Atlantic was nothing new when the *Titanic* made impact. Icebergs had been a hazard ever since ships and boats started to make their tentative way across the ocean, and the fog prevalent on the North American side of the Atlantic at certain times of the year was an extra hazard, hiding the 'bergs from view. However, the *Titanic* disaster, where around 1,200 lives were lost, illustrated the greatly increased risk of the higher speeds of passenger ships to maintain schedules that did not allow slowing down in iceberg-risk areas.

Speed is the problem

At slow speed, an iceberg does not present a significant danger because, even in fog, it can usually be detected before contact is made. It was only when steamships started to go faster than 10 knots that icebergs became hazardous. It took the *Titanic* disaster to get that danger really appreciated. One of the most significant resulting developments was the creation of the International Ice Patrol (IIP). Set up in 1913, it put out ships dedicated to locating icebergs as they drifted south into the shipping lanes. Today there are patrols by aircraft to locate the positions of icebergs, with satellite pictures slowly taking over, so that icebergs are now carefully monitored. This allows ships to take avoiding action long before it becomes urgent. Each year the IIP establishes a Limit of All Known Ice. The hope is that if ships keep outside this area then they will not be at risk from icebergs.

Most of the icebergs are found in the spring and summer, in the area off the coast of Newfoundland, further north up towards Greenland and out into the Atlantic. The icebergs break away from the 100 or so glaciers that extend from the Greenland ice cap on the west coast. They then drift south on the Labrador Current, slowly melting as they encounter warmer waters. It is estimated that around 15,000 icebergs calve each year. The total travel of an average iceberg is around 1,800 miles and it can take up to three years before they reach the North Atlantic shipping lanes. Icebergs are rare at anywhere below 45 degrees north, but there is a measure of unpredictability that makes mariners very wary of them, and they have been seen around the Azores. The danger of icebergs is unique to the North Atlantic, and as one of the busiest shipping areas in the world the risk is considerable, although under control thanks to the work of the IIP. However, as more and more ships visit the Antarctic regions the same problem is developing there, albeit on a smaller scale.

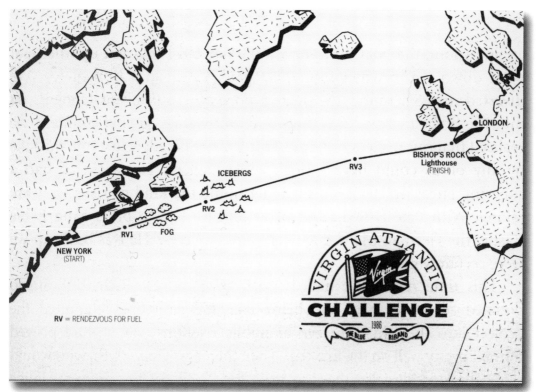

Cape Race: this route across the Atlantic took us right through the main iceberg area – this was also where we could expect to find fog.

An iceberg park

When we made the Virgin Atlantic crossings, the threat of icebergs presented us with a real challenge. To set a record, we obviously wanted to take the shortest possible route. That took us well north, up the Eastern Seaboard of the US and Canada to Cape Race, and round the south-east corner of Newfoundland. Cape Race is a sort of crossroads for icebergs and the area where they are most prevalent. This is the point where they come down the channel between Greenland and the Canadian coast; they then tend to spread out across the northern Atlantic as they come under the influence of the Gulf Stream. Those that come down close inshore off Labrador and Newfoundland tend to get sucked into an eddy of the Labrador Current, which sweeps around the bottom corner of Newfoundland.

This means that there is a sort of iceberg parking lot just south of Cape Race; right on the route we wanted to take. We had to find our way through this mess of icebergs if we were to stick to our plan of taking the shortest route and I had to come up with a solution that allowed a safe passage when running at 50 knots. We did not want to end up as another *Titanic*.

It was not so much the big icebergs that concerned me, because they would show up on radar at sufficient distance to avoid them. I was much more worried about the bergy bits and the growlers around the icebergs, the debris that drops off the 'berg as it melts. These lumps of ice, which can be anything from 2 to 20m across, are not a major problem for large ships operating at moderate speeds, but could spell disaster for a small fast boat like ours. We could have chosen the longer route and avoided them altogether, but I felt more research might throw up a solution. What I wanted to know was where these lumps of

An aircraft of the International Ice Patrol locating icebergs in the North Atlantic. Satellites are increasingly being used for this purpose.

ice would lie in relation to the main iceberg, but I could find nothing in the textbooks that would help.

It was only when flying across the Atlantic on one of the Virgin Atlantic aircraft, looking down on the ice, that I discovered the secret. It was quite logical really. An iceberg, sticking well up above the water level, has much more windage than the small lumps of ice surrounding it, which are virtually awash. This means that an iceberg will go downwind faster than the small lumps of ice. If we wanted to avoid the small lumps, we simply needed to pass the iceberg on its leeward or downwind side. All the small ice would be up to windward, travelling slower than the main berg. In practice, we tried to give the bergs as wide a margin as possible just in case. Ice and fast boats do not mix and, frankly, it was a bit scary to see six icebergs on the radar when travelling at speed in thick fog. Record breaking is never easy.

Ice comes in many forms

For most seamen, icebergs are the main hazard created by cold conditions, but ice comes in many forms and can create some very unexpected dangers which have troubled sailors over the centuries. In the past, the cold regions of the world tended to be off the beaten track as far as sea travel was concerned, but fishermen journeyed into these ice regions in search of the prolific fish and whales that could be found there. What must it have been like back in the 16th and 17th centuries when fleets of sailing fishing boats travelled across the Atlantic to catch cod on the Grand Banks? These vessels, which were probably no more than 100ft in length, were entirely alone and without support from land, and large numbers of them didn't make it back. Getting into trouble in those icy waters was likely to spell instant death, but many thought the risk worthwhile because of the rich rewards.

Clearing the ice build-up on a ship to help restore stability.

Ice can cause capsize

I was up in the inhospitable waters north of Iceland in the winter of 1975/6, when Britain and Iceland were fighting over fishing rights there. It is such wild country that it is considered a good day when only a force 8 gale is blowing. The Icelanders had their rather fragile gunboats to take on the fishing boats, while I was on a very large tug, the *Lloydsman*, the sort of tough ship needed for these hostile waters. The cod war was not fought with guns. Our job was to keep between the gunboats and the fishing fleet, so that the gunboats could not harm the fishing vessels. Frankly, it would have been safer to fire guns at each other rather than suffer the collisions we had in those wild seas. But it was our common enemy, ice, that proved most dangerous. When the ships started to ice up from the spray freezing on deck, we all knew it was time to head south as fast as possible to reduce the ice load and the possibility of capsizing.

On one occasion, ice built up on a part of the superstructure where it was difficult to access to chip the ice off. As we headed south to warmer waters the whole lump of ice suddenly broke away from the vertical surface and crashed to the deck. The estimated 20 tonnes of ice crashing down proved too much for the deck, which split. Suddenly we had a serious problem: not the risk of capsize but the risk of water entering the hull from the split deck. Fortunately the hole was not large and was easily blocked, but our experience shows just how ice can produce many unexpected consequences.

Unexpected problems

When I was working with Trinity House on their lighthouse tenders I encountered many of the unforeseen problems caused by cold and ice. During the winter of 1963 it was extremely cold for many weeks, with the wind howling down from the north and areas of the North Sea starting to freeze over. The ship I was on was dedicated to servicing the buoys and lights in the Thames Estuary region and here the ice became a severe problem. Sheets of ice the size of a football pitch drifted out from the estuary; a whole new experience for me. These floes did not really trouble the ship, which simply ploughed through the relatively thin ice. It was when back in harbour and tied up to a buoy that we realised the problem: we could not get ashore because we could not lower our boat into the water, only onto the ice that surrounded the ship.

That winter caused us a real headache because the navigation buoys we needed to service were icing up. Spray was being blown over the cage superstructure of the buoy and when this froze it made the buoy so top-heavy that it capsized. It was a major task to lift these 3-tonne buoys in their capsized state, and then chip the ice away to restore the buoy to its former, useful glory with the light working too. This became a full-time job because the buoys would ice up again within a few days and the whole process needed repeating.

With over 200 buoys to service, you can imagine what a job it was. However, shipping was still active in even these conditions and we had to try to keep the navigation channels open. Looking back I am surprised that we did not have any cases of hypothermia among the crews working on deck in these extreme conditions. It was a nightmare scenario and opens your eyes to just how much the world changes in extreme cold conditions.

Not much more ice and the buoy will topple.

Ice on a small boat

I saw just how dangerous extreme cold can be when I was booked for a small boat passage down the east coast of the United States. I should have known from past experience that this might not prove to be the interesting trip I anticipated. However, it was a journey I had always wanted to do and I jumped at the chance without thinking too much about the consequences. The boat was a Little Harbor 44: a smart 40-knot 44-footer built in traditional New England style. We planned to start off from Rhode Island (between New York and Boston) and head right down to Florida on a trip scheduled to last a week. There is something exciting about the prospect of leaving the cold of the north and heading towards the sunshine of Florida. I should have known better.

The first hint of trouble came when I stepped off the aircraft at Providence in Rhode Island. I could hardly catch my breath in the extreme cold. I had flown transatlantic that day and switched planes in New York for the commuter flight up to Providence. The airline managed to lose my bag during the transfer, so I was in the bitter cold with just my casual travelling clothes. They promised to deliver the bag the next day, but by then I would be off at sea after an early morning start. At the crack of dawn I was picked up by the other two crew, who generously lent me some of their warm clothes.

It took over an hour just to thaw out the boat and clear the windscreen. Then we set off, hoping that the heat from the engines would keep the boat and us warm, while keeping the outside cold at bay. That was when the nightmare started. The spray generated by the hull was freezing on the outside of the windscreen and the moisture from our breath was freezing on the inside. This meant we had to stop

Ice can stop your GPS and other electronics from working.

and clear both at frequent intervals, but it gradually improved as the boat warmed up. As we got out into the open sea the more serious problems began.

First of all, the GPS antenna iced up and we lost our position information. This was quite serious as many of the navigation marks weren't working in the cold. With hindsight we should have taken this as a warning of worse to come and turned back. Next, the radar suffered from the same problem, but lack of navigation information was soon a minor problem in comparison with how the boat was icing up. In open waters with a fresh breeze, there was a lot of spray and the foredeck was quickly covered with ice, which made going out on deck treacherous. The handrails were twice their normal size with ice, making a grip unreliable. The worst discovery was that the aft cockpit was also full of ice, adding considerable weight to the boat. All this happened within an hour and it was frightening just how quickly the situation was deteriorating. It was time to find the nearest harbour and a measure of safety, but just trying to tie the boat up in those conditions was perilous. I knew a slip would mean death, as it was near impossible to recover from a dip in those icy waters. Without previous experience it was difficult to assess just how bad things were, but we should never have left in those conditions and it was two days before we got going again. Just enough time for my luggage to catch up with me.

Fighting our way through the ice in New York Harbour. The ice made it difficult to get to refuelling docks.

Trapped

Ice comes in all shapes and sizes and creates many problems, some of which are difficult to anticipate without experience. Get it wrong in cold or ice and disaster looms. There is very little room for negotiation, the ice holds all the aces, and you start from a position of extreme weakness. Polar exploration in wooden sailing ships, such as the search for the Northwest Passage, must have been traumatic in the extreme. The prospect of wintering when trapped in the ice is something that few would contemplate these days. Just imagine being locked in the ice for months on end, knowing that you had to rely entirely on your own resources, and knowing that no one could come to your aid if the ship got into trouble. It was Shackleton who demonstrated just how difficult it was to escape from Antarctic waters with his epic small-boat voyage, but as with most disasters we only hear the tales of those who make it home.

Unsinkable?

Another ship that was hailed as unsinkable sank off the southern tip of Greenland after hitting an iceberg in 1959. The *Hedtoft* was built as an ice-class ship, yet when she hit the iceberg she sank, and all 55 passengers and 40 crew died in the incident. Another ship built to ice-standards went aground off the coast of Greenland in 1972, but suffered less damage. The 52 passengers were taken off and the ship was refloated.

Today, as cruise ships increasingly head into the Polar Region to allow passengers to view the last great wilderness, the way is wide open for a disaster of epic proportions to occur. We have already seen cruise ships grounding in the Antarctic and being abandoned. Experience shows just how difficult it can be to rescue people from ships in these regions. What is not fully recognised is that conventional lifesaving equipment on ships is not likely to be much use on ice and there is no alternative on offer.

Cruise ship incidents

An accident like this could have been so much worse, as it could have been for MS *Explorer*. In 2007 the cruise ship hit an iceberg in the Antarctic during the night. The reports say that the ship had a relatively small hole in the hull and this perhaps explains the comparatively slow rate of ingress of

The cruise liner Explorer *lies on its side in the ice floes before sinking after striking an iceberg.*

The open lifeboats from the Explorer did not offer the survivors any protection from the cold.

water into the hull. The disturbing question is, if this was a relatively small hole, why did the ship sink? Passenger ships are supposed to be subdivided, so that they will remain afloat and stable even if two compartments are flooded. Compartments are defined as the space between each watertight bulkhead, but may be subdivided longitudinally as well. Whatever the situation with the *Explorer,* it looks as though the watertight doors, which need to be closed to maintain the ship's integrity, were not shut. The ship should not have sunk with only a relatively small hole in the hull, which shouldn't have extended beyond the two compartments. Reports also suggest that the engine room became flooded because the power went off, and that the ship was then seen going astern when apparently the engines started up again. It is all a big mystery, but sounds as though this ship was operating in ice regions, when not fully equipped for the job.

Despite the danger of having to abandon ship at night as the *Explorer* listed over further and further (before finally sinking), all the passengers and crew took to the lifeboats in what seems like an orderly evacuation and, amazingly, spent five hours in open lifeboats waiting for rescue.

What is a ship operating in very cold regions doing with just open lifeboats on board, where the risk of severe exposure is very high? Those passengers and crew were lucky that they had time to don exposure suits before abandoning ship, and doing this ensured their survival, but what if there had been the need for a much more hasty evacuation? What if the seas around the iceberg had been ice-covered, making the launch of the lifeboats more difficult and risky? What if there had not been another cruise ship only a few hours away, ready to come to the rescue? The passengers and crew were very lucky in this drama, which could so easily have resulted in a considerable loss of life.

In both of these incidents the ships involved were relatively small, with only a modest number of passengers on board. The worry comes when the large cruise ships visit these hostile regions, as they are starting to do in increasing numbers. Picture the scenario of a cruise ship carrying over 3,000 passengers, and finding itself in trouble in these remote areas. It is interesting to see that the companies selling these cruises label their ships 'ice-proof', when in fact they have no ice classification at all and the hulls are only built to the standards required for normal shipping. Ice classification requires a considerably stronger hull. The trouble is that there doesn't seem to be a regulatory body that can rule that these ships must not visit polar waters. Nor is there a body who can dictate what can or

Are passenger ships taking too many risks by taking their passengers up close to glaciers?

Photograph: http://community.netidea.com/teekay

cannot be done with cruise ships, or any other ships for that matter. As a spokesperson for the British Antarctic Survey said, 'None of the huge ships is ice strengthened, and if there were a problem there could be a very significant disaster with substantial loss of life.'

Uncharted waters

Another problem for the ships that wander off the beaten track into ice regions is that they are moving further and further into uncharted waters. As the areas of ice-covered seas recede each year with global warming, the recession uncovers waters that have not been surveyed at all, or for which the survey data is likely to be unreliable. Any ship venturing into these relatively uncharted waters puts itself at risk, but the demand to take passengers into new areas means that they seem prepared to do this. Cruise ships are at the forefront of this exploration, but yachts and fishing boats are not far behind and growing numbers are to be found in both the Arctic and Antarctic, exploring what is virtually virgin territory. Yachts possibly have a better chance of coping with uncharted waters than ships. They are much more manoeuvrable, and navigate much as the explorers of old did, relying on good eyesight and heaving-to at night. The worry is that these modern-day explorers will expect some sort of rescue attempt if they do get into trouble.

It isn't just cruise ships operating in the polar regions that have a problem with unsuitable lifesaving equipment. In the Baltic and adjacent waters, ferries still operate in the winter months, cutting their own channels through the sea ice. In many cases the ice has already been broken by the passage of earlier ships, leaving a mass of large lumps that do not cause a problem for the ships themselves, but which would make it virtually impossible for lifeboats and liferafts to operate effectively. Normal shore-based lifeboats would also be ineffective in these conditions and the only means of rescue is likely to rely on icebreakers, other ships or helicopters. It seems that nobody wants to acknowledge the problem of operating in icy waters, because they would then be forced to do something about it.

One oil company has done something about the problems of rescue in ice regions, because it was the only way it could get a licence to exploit the oil reserves in these inhospitable areas. The solution was found in tracked vehicles that could operate both on ice and in the water, and make the transition from one to the other. It is not a complete solution, as these vehicles cannot transverse all types of ice and water. They provide only a temporary refuge, but it is a step in the right direction. Similarly, ordinary ship's lifeboats have comparable limitations in the open sea, but create a temporary refuge that can buy time. However, this oil rig survival vehicle is an expensive solution and thus not likely to prove viable for the large numbers of passengers on a cruise ship.

Experience vs unpredictability

For most seamen, ice is an unknown quantity and they lack the resources or experience to deal with it. Take the case of the Russian icebreaker, *Aleksey Maryshev,* which had been converted into a cruise ship to give passengers the possibility of close encounters in ice regions. This ice-strengthened vessel went close to the 30m tall Hornsund Glacier on Spitzbergen, to give the passengers a close-up view. It was reported that it was some 50m away when the glacier calved, showering the ship with blocks of ice. Naturally, most of the passengers were out on deck at the time admiring the view; nine of them had to be flown to hospital, some with serious injuries.

It would be reasonable to think that an icebreaker crew would have some experience of ice conditions and would have been aware of the risks of getting close to the face of a glacier. They had a lucky escape: the ship survived, and despite the injuries none of the passengers died, but it was a close call. The tour operator said that this was the first incident that they had experienced in 23 years of operating tours in polar regions, which demonstrates the danger of complacency. This is the type of occurrence that should ring alarm bells in the halls of authority, but where are these halls? Who can set the limits and who will enforce them? Perhaps the insurance companies, who stand to lose the most, should be taking a more proactive role in ensuring safety in these inhospitable regions.

One small step in the right direction has been the requirement that all shipping operating in higher latitudes must have exposure suits on board. This is why those on board the *Explorer* survived. Exposure suits allow survivors to cope with cold conditions for much longer, even if in icy water. The only problem is that these suits can take a minute or more to put on and they restrict mobility, factors that could be significant for the crew of a smaller vessel that is sinking rapidly.

These problems will only become more apparent as increasing numbers of passengers demand to visit wilderness areas, but also as global warming opens up areas for cruise ships that were previously impassable. The Northwest Passage is a case in point, and as things stand this could be open to shipping during the summer months within a few years. Transiting the Northwest Passage would certainly make a great cruise ship itinerary, but how will cruise ships fare if things go wrong in an area where search and rescue facilities do not exist? What if one of these ships caught fire? Perhaps the heat would melt the ice and allow lifeboats to be launched, but these days most ships rely on outside help when things go awry and that help could be many miles away.

Where the cruise ships go, the more daring yachtsman is likely to follow and some are already heading into both the Arctic and the Antarctic. There is a desire for adventure that reflects the motives of the explorers of old, and these cold regions provide one of the few remaining areas where there is a true wilderness. Perhaps there is more hope here because any yachtsman who ventures into the Arctic or Antarctic regions is likely to be equipped for the job and maybe is not likely to expect rescue if things go wrong. Operating in ice is such an unpredictable matter. The ships and boats may be strengthened to withstand the impact of colliding with the ice, but the safety margins will be greatly reduced and consequently the risks higher. If ships and boats can get into trouble in quite routine operations in the more benign waters of moderate latitudes, then it is not difficult to imagine how the problems could mount in more severe conditions where exposure can be a major threat and help is far away.

An ice-breaking ship ploughs through relatively thin ice.

MARINE ACCIDENT INVESTIGATION BRANCH

Ice can be a problem even in the UK

Narrative

A small wooden-hulled pleasure cruiser was manoeuvring within a marina on the Norfolk Broads. It was early in the morning on a particularly cold winter's day. The air temperature was about –4 degrees C.

The craft struck ice, which proved to be much thicker and therefore stronger than the skipper expected.

This caused serious damage to the hull planks, which was not immediately obvious to the skipper as he continued to manoeuvre the craft. As the vessel began to take on water he realised the seriousness of the situation.

The skipper was able to secure the vessel to a marina berth, but not in time to save the vessel, which sank in about 15ft of water. During the sinking, the attached ropes broke and the craft drifted off into the main channel.

Around 80 litres of diesel oil, 6 litres of engine sump oil and 5 litres of paraffin were released into the Broads. The Environment Agency and the Broads Authority attended. The vessel was salvaged the following day.

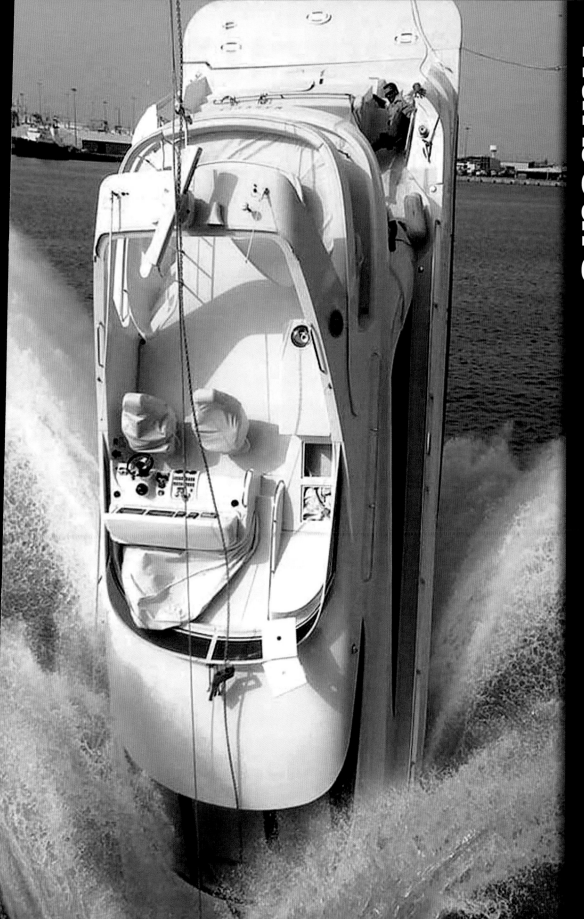

The bulk carrier Pasha Bulker *aground near a harbour entrance in Australia.*

Harbours

If you think that harbours are a haven from disaster then think again. Probably more disasters occur in harbour than ever happen out in the open sea, but because of the proximity to help they don't usually result in the same dire consequences. It is quite logical that more disasters happen in or on the approaches to harbour because it is here that the dangers of shallow water, rocks and other vessels all become much closer. Failure of any of the on-board systems will have more immediate consequences in the close-quarters situation of a harbour. Add to that the dangers inherent in handling some cargoes and the fact that crews will often relax their guard once in the apparent safety of harbour and things can quickly go wrong.

Entering harbour

Coming into harbour from seaward can be quite challenging, particularly if you're unfamiliar with the harbour. This is the time when the wide open spaces of the open ocean are left behind and you are faced with channels that get progressively narrower and shallower, rocks that become progressively closer, and other vessels that may pass just yards rather than miles away. The land seems to close in on you; up ahead an entrance can look impossibly narrow and your own vessel can seem far larger than normal. Preparation is the key to getting in safely, but translating what is on the chart into what lies ahead can lead to unwelcome and frightening surprises. The situation is compounded in the dark when your supposedly guiding lights can be lost against a background of flashing neon signs and small craft moving about.

Bigger ships and smaller margins

One might think that detailed electronic information and guidance systems would come to the rescue, but the truth is that few harbours want to invest in these systems to help small craft, and for big ships any advance in these systems is used to expand the size of vessels that can use the approach channels, rather than increase safety levels. Ports and harbour authorities are, in the main, profit-making organisations. None want to be left behind in the race to handle larger and larger ships, so they try to pare down safety margins, such as the depth of water under the vessel and the distance off dangers. A deep draft ship coming in through a narrow channel with only a few feet under its keel has very little room to manoeuvre if things go wrong.

Cruise ships are lucrative visitors to harbours and are seldom turned away. I have seen a large cruise ship being brought in backwards through a narrow rocky channel into a small harbour. There was no room to swing this ship inside the harbour, so it was done outside and then came in stern first, under its own power and without tug assistance. You have to admire the handling skills of the pilot on that ship and the wonderful manoeuvrability, but the margins for error in that operation were worryingly small.

The superyacht Lady Maura *went aground on rocks outside Monaco Harbour, making a very public mistake in front of the rich and famous of this Riviera town.*

A big ship in a little harbour. The safety margins can be very tight when harbour authorities try to exploit the limits of what a harbour can handle.

The following is an indication of how tight things can get. A channel was developed in Holyhead harbour to accommodate the new high-speed ferry service between Holyhead and Dublin. The new ferries were some of the largest high-speed ferries ever built and they were a very tight fit in the narrow twisting channel. An electronic control system was developed that took full automatic control of the ferry and guided it into its berth without human intervention. This was considered safer than relying on human control. Is this a sign of things to come in narrow harbour channels? I can see the attraction of minimising the cost of dredging new channels and facilities, but what sort of safety margin is acceptable? Who dictates what is and what is not an acceptable risk for shipping in harbours?

Operations concerned with bringing ships into harbour are often not planned with adequate safety margins to cope when things go wrong, and there are many tales of ships and yachts suffering mechanical failure of one sort or another when entering or leaving harbour. I have experienced it a couple of times in my sea-going career. On one occasion one of the engineering crew shut off the steam supply to the steering engine that controlled the rudder. After the surprise of finding that the ship was not responding to the helm, we attempted to find a solution. On this occasion a tug towed us off and we carried on up the channel. The grounding was on soft mud so no damage was done, but it doesn't take a lot of imagination to see the same thing happening to a ship loaded with oil, where the seabed is not so friendly.

Electrical failure

A much more serious accident resulted from an electrical failure on board a fast ferry in Hong Kong. The failure put the throttles and steering out of action, but the problem was compounded because the throttles were left wide open with no system to bring them back to neutral, and thus no easy way to stop the engines. The ferry careered across the harbour, eventually hitting the shore at full speed, killing seven people on board. Seven deaths because no one had done a 'what if' assessment of the systems on board the ferry. This is something that is well worth doing on board any yacht. The assumption is often that the builder will have completed this check, but don't bank on it.

Dangerous cargoes

Things were a lot worse for the *Exxon Valdez,* a big tanker that grounded as she was leaving the port of Valdez in Alaska fully laden with crude oil. This accident was caused by a navigation error and shows the scale of disaster that can result from getting it wrong in harbour channels. The resulting pollution is still affecting the ecology of the region today, 20 years after the event. The risks of large tankers and ships carrying liquid gas going aground or having engine or steering failure in the approaches to harbours are now more recognised. Most ports handling these ships now require them to have escort tugs, specially designed powerful tugs that are attached to the stern of the ship and can act as a brake if things go wrong. It is a costly solution, but does seem to be effective when handling ships with dangerous cargoes in confined waters.

The **Exxon Valdez** *is still causing pollution, 20 years after going aground.*

At present these gas carriers rely mainly on a containment system whereby the gas is cooled to very low temperatures that convert it into a liquid. However, there is a new generation of gas ships where the gas is transported under pressure, and this could create a whole new level of risk in harbour. Most Liquefied Natural Gas (LNG) terminals are being established in remote areas to minimise public reaction against them, but the records show there have already been over 20 accidents involving LNG ships. Only one of these was a major accident: the collision between an LNG ship and a US submarine in the Straits of Gibraltar in 2002. Fortunately the gas ship was empty. What has not been considered in analysis of the risks is the possibility of terrorist threats and suicide bombing attacks, such as that on the USS *Cole* in Aden Harbour. Gas ships must look like a prime target for those wanting to cause maximum impact and damage.

When a laden tanker is involved in a grounding or collision, it is pollution that causes most concern, but what if the pilot or captain misjudges and collides with the oil terminal where he is berthing? The risk would then be of fire or possibly explosion. The situation would be even worse with a ship carrying liquid gas. Liquid gases are highly inflammable as they boil off, but they are also heavier than air and can therefore spread across a harbour. Then, it only needs one spark to set things off. Moreover, should gas leak out from a penetration of one of the tanks, the contact of the very cold liquid gas with seawater can be explosive in its own right. As the liquid gas hits the relatively warm water it vaporises and as gas takes up 600 times more space than it does in liquid form there is a very sudden and explosive expansion. It is reckoned that this initial explosive expansion would be enough to cause further damage, possibly leading to a catastrophic failure of the containing tank. A major fire would almost certainly follow, in a disaster that would probably go down as one of the worst in maritime history. One study suggests a fireball extending out seven miles from the original point of contact.

I cannot find any record of such a disaster taking place to date, but considering the expected surge in the amount of liquid gas being transported over the next 10 years, it seems inevitable that tragedy will occur, and most likely in harbour. There has been a huge expansion in the numbers and the size of these gas tankers as the world's demand for gas expands at a rapid rate. At the time of writing, there are 220 of these ships in operation and another 134 on order.

Carrying explosives

An example of what can happen when ships with dangerous cargoes are in harbour occurred in 1917 during the first World War, when the city of Halifax in Nova Scotia was devastated. A French ship fully loaded with 2,653 tonnes of wartime explosives had a collision in the harbour; the ship exploded, killing more than 2,000 people. Until the atomic bomb was developed, this was the largest man-made explosion ever recorded.

It was at 08:40 in the morning that the French cargo ship *Mont Blanc* collided with the Norwegian cargo ship *Imo* in the entrance channel to Halifax Harbour. Ten minutes later the *Mont Blanc* caught fire. Seeing the flames on board and knowing what their cargo was, the crew

All buildings and structures along a mile of shore adjacent to the exploded ship were obliterated.

abandoned ship and left it drifting. Not knowing the *Mont Blanc* contained explosives, other ships attempted to tackle the fire and take the *Mont Blanc* in tow. The ship eventually drifted alongside a pier, starting a fire there, and thousands of people turned out on shore to watch the drama. Twenty-five minutes after the fire broke out, the explosion occurred and the effect was devastating. It caused a mini tsunami in the harbour that was estimated at 59ft high. The pressure wave from the explosion flattened buildings and trees and started further fires. An area with a radius of 1 mile around the explosion site was flattened and the boom was heard over 200 miles away.

The Second World War produced more than one major harbour disaster story. When the Germans bombed Bari Harbour in Southern Italy, the port was crowded with ships. The story goes that one of these was loaded with secret mustard-gas bombs. Reports suggest that over 1,000 servicemen died, as did an equal number of civilians ashore, and that is simply from poisoning, rather than the effects of the explosion.

The Texas City disaster in 1947 occurred when two ships in harbour had cargoes containing ammonium nitrate. A fire started in one ship, the *Grandcamp,* and despite efforts to fight the fire, the cargo exploded. The shock of the explosion was felt 250 miles away. It was 15 hours later that a second ship, the *High Flyer,* also exploded after being set alight by the *Grandcamp.* The official figures put the death toll at 581 people and, like the Halifax explosion, there were reports of a mini tsunami in the harbour.

Britain has its own potential explosive disaster in the form of the wreck of the *Richard Montgomery.* This American ship was loaded with 1,500 tonnes of munitions when it sank in the Thames Estuary in 1944. Due to the risk of explosion, the wreck has been left undisturbed ever since and nobody really knows what state the explosives are in. When I worked for Trinity House we would lay wreck buoys at each end of the ship; there was always a considerable sense of relief when we finished the job and steamed away. If this load of explosives ever went off the results would probably match the Halifax explosion. As there is an oil refinery and an LNG terminal not many miles away, the disaster could snowball.

With so many ships carrying such dangerous cargoes into harbours, a chain reaction of disasters becomes increasingly feasible. When I made enquiries into how ports and harbours have prepared for and analysed the risks of this, I met with a wall of silence. The most expansive would only say that every harbour has its own contingency plans for emergencies.

The wreck of the **Richard Montgomery** *can be seen above water, and below with a sonar image.*

Ships damage harbours

Ships are notorious for damaging harbour facilities. When a large ship is moving in harbour it will do so very slowly, but even so there is a huge momentum involved if the ship comes into contact with a fixed object. Jetties and wharves are very solidly built, but are not designed to withstand the force of a fully laden ship coming alongside at anything over a barely discernible speed. Most harbours have stories of facilities being damaged by ships, but it is the consequential damage, when the harbour facility is put out of action, that can have the most serious effect.

Probably more at risk are ferry terminals, where many ferries may dock every day. A Ro-Ro ferry terminal that allows vehicles to drive on and off is a very fragile structure compared with the weight of the ship berthing alongside, so if the captain makes an error damage can result. One ship trying to berth at a Ro-Ro ramp in Ireland got itself in a mess and overshot the terminal. It ended up in a marina where it destroyed much of the facility and sunk many yachts. This damage was a consequence of trying to fit too many facilities into a compact harbour.

This is the bow of the container ship Maersk Tampa *after it rammed the quay wall in Oakland, USA.*

Two Maersk container ships managed to T-bone the same quay, in the same port, when undertaking the same manoeuvre. Both ships were turning off the quay so that they could berth with the alternative side alongside, when they ran straight into the quay wall. The *Maersk Tampa* was the first to carry out this manoeuvre at the container terminal in the Port of Oakland, California. Then six months later, the *Glasgow Maersk* did exactly the same thing. In both cases the bow of the ship was severely damaged, the plating peeling back like opening a can of beans.

The result of hitting a jetty when manoeuvring in harbour.

Mechanical failure

Most disasters that occur in harbour are due to some sort of mechanical failure. One such incident occurred in Karachi Harbour when I was working on a cargo ship. It was going to be a simple operation, shifting the ship from one berth to another to start loading cargo. We had a tug in attendance tied up to the bow to help with the manoeuvre as there was a strong wind blowing. It should have been a routine operation, but the tug line parted at a critical moment. This allowed the bow of the ship to swing in towards the quay and we hit the stonework with a bang. And that was the least of our problems. Because we hit the quay at an angle, the flare of the bow was overhanging by quite an amount and at just that point stood one of the tall dockside cranes. These

Handling heavy-lift cargoes can be a risky operation. It was an expensive mistake dropping this 500 tonne unit.

cranes are designed to be stable when handling cargo, but they are not designed to be hit by ships. Consequently, when our ship made contact with the crane, it tilted over and seemed to hang for an eternity, balancing on just one set of wheels. Then, ever so slowly, it toppled over away from the quay to hit the adjacent cargo shed and plunge through its roof. Fortunately no one was in the way. That broken rope caused damage that cost in the region of £1 million to repair.

The largest container ship

It seems that container ships even start their lives in trouble in harbour. The *Emma Maersk,* the largest container ship in the world, caught fire when she was under construction at the Odense Shipyard in Denmark. Welding was taking place in the engine room when sparks ignited some wooden pallets. The fire spread rapidly through the accommodation and up to the bridge, and the whole superstructure of the ship had to be replaced. Amazingly this only delayed the completion of the ship by a couple of months. The *Emma Maersk* is close to 400m long, making her one of the largest ships in the world. She is fitted with the largest diesel engine ever built, pushing out 109,000hp to give a speed of 25.5 knots, making her faster than most passenger ships.

Yet another ship was in a collision in the River Schelde, near Antwerp in Belgium. The *Maersk Bahrain* collided with another container ship, the *Pelican 1*, and in this case it was the *Pelican* that suffered most, needing to be grounded when the engine room flooded. The River Schelde, with its long estuary, is a common place for collisions and grounding. The container ship *Fowairet* grounded there in 2005, causing serious hull damage. Another collision occurred when a tanker was leaving the Botlek Dock area in nearby Rotterdam. The tanker *Hellenic Star* lost its steering at a critical moment and collided with the passing container ship *Western Trader*. The *Western Trader* was grounded to avoid sinking, once again showing how small the safety margins can be in a busy harbour.

Yachts get it wrong in harbour as well and most marinas tell stories of yachtsmen who have made a mistake with the controls when berthing, causing considerable damage. While not in the same league as the damage caused by ships, these incidents can cause injury as well as the damage to the boat and the pride of the person driving. We all assume that everything will go according to plan and that the controls of the yacht will respond as expected. But as we switch more and more to electronic control, there is always the risk that the software could play up at a critical moment. I saw this on a big power catamaran in Fort Lauderdale in Florida. The thrust from four engines was combined into water jet propulsion, with the whole thing controlled by computer. As we were about to pass through the narrow gap of one of the lifting bridges, the computer went down and we ended up going through sideways before we could get the backup system running. That was a scary, narrow escape; a collision with that bridge could have put both the bridge and the boat out of action.

Yacht and ship incidents

Collisions between yachts and ships are becoming a feature of the marine world and the vast majority of these collisions take place within the confines of a harbour. In these waters the vessels are operating much closer to each other than within a port, and it is usually safe to assume that it is the yacht that has made the errors. The ship may have very little room to manoeuvre in the narrow channels and, no matter what the Collision Regulations (Colregs) say, it makes sense for a yacht to keep out of the way of a ship. A surprising number of yachts do not seem to realise that they should not come within 100m of a moving ship. The Italian delegation to the International Marine Organisation (IMO) provided the statistic that there were 65 collisions between yachts and ships over a five-year period in Italian waters. That does not sound a lot and there were only two resulting fatalities, but this has led to the Italian authorities making proposals that would demand all leisure craft keep clear of commercial ships both inside harbours and on the open ocean.

Some harbours provide separate channels for use by small craft, while others provide a patrol boat escort to keep small craft at a distance when a ship is moving. These arrangements suggest that a problem does exist in some harbours. A yacht is certain to come off worse in any encounter of this type. I wonder how many of the reported incidents come about because the yacht has suffered an engine or steering failure at a critical moment. Sometimes it can seem that yachts have little idea of the danger when they see a big ship entering harbour; to get a better view, they want to get as close as possible.

This American tug has two engines for greater manoeuvrability.

The role of tugs

Tugs play a vital role in ensuring the safety of ships moving around a harbour, but the tugs themselves are also at risk in some of the operations. Older types of tug were designed to pull from the stern and if the tow rope moved around to the side they were in danger of capsizing. Many of these older tugs only had a single propeller and so could not manoeuvre away without compounding the problem. The safety was in the hands of the skipper and the only real solution was to slip the tow, but that might endanger the ship. Modern tugs are much more manoeuvrable; the power of their engines can be used to move the tug back to the correct angle to the tow rope.

In Liverpool's Birkenhead Docks, the tug *Thorngarth* was helping to berth a ship as it approached the locks when they collided. The *Thorngarth* was the bow tug and another tug was attached to the stern. As the *Thorngarth* picked up the tow line it ended up across the bows of the ship and this caused significant damage to the tug, but only minor damage to the ship, which was fortunate, as it carried a cargo of chemicals. This accident was blamed largely on the tug master's lack of familiarity with the *Thorngarth*.

Fog can create severe difficulties for harbour operations and adds a new dimension to the risk to ships.

Approaching in fog

The River Mersey has had its fair share of accidents, including a recent collision between a fast ferry and a cargo ship. This took place in thick fog, when the ferry was approaching its berth after a passage from the Isle of Man. The cargo ship *Alaska Rainbow* was heading for Birkenhead Docks and was being controlled by two tugs. The ferry *Sea Express 1* was under the command of a trainee captain and took avoiding action when one of the tugs appeared out of the fog. It then took further avoiding action when the *Alaska Rainbow* emerged, but it was too late and the resulting collision tore a large hole in the side of the aluminium *Sea Express 1*. The ferry began listing, but was towed to safety and the 258 passengers disembarked. You have to wonder about the effectiveness of the radar watch on board these ships and the role of the vessel traffic service that was monitoring shipping in the estuary in this situation. Navigating in harbours in thick fog seems to be an accepted practice today in order to meet schedules, but the risks can increase dramatically in poor visibility.

Pilots can only advise

Such events are often more professionally embarrassing than dangerous, but there are many more serious events that result in considerable damage, injury and death. What is surprising is that very often the ships have pilots on board who should be familiar with the port and its approaches. However, pilots have a very difficult role to play. They are primarily on board to advise, but in effect operate the ship with the captain monitoring progress. It is a sound system that works most of the time but pilots often operate under very difficult conditions and these have been compounded by the introduction of advanced electronic systems.

A pilot may go on board a different ship every day of his working life, and is expected to be immediately familiar with the bridge layout and all the systems there. I have spoken to pilots who complain that the operating systems for each manufacturer's radar are different, and they have no time to familiarise themselves with the controls before they must use them. Some ports are now developing electronic systems that the pilot brings on board to help with the navigation, so that he can rely on his own information.

Small wonder, though, that there is a long history of pilots being blamed for mistakes when ships get into trouble in harbours. Pilots have to rely on the ship's crew doing the right things and that does not always happen. Take the case of the *Crimson Mars* when she was leaving harbour on the River Tamar in Australia. The pilot ordered the helm to be put hard to port, but instead the helmsman put the helm to starboard at a critical point in the river passage. It was a minute before the mistake was realised and by that time collision was inevitable. The ship hit a reef and as a result she was badly holed in the bow. This was a simple human error and the pilot got the blame for not monitoring the helmsman's actions. In his defence the pilot said he was placed in an impossible situation, because from the position where he could see out of the bridge windows, he could not also see the rudder indicator.

Slow down in fog?

Pilots were on board two ships that collided in the River Humber in 2006. This collision between two cargo ships demonstrates the over-reliance on radar prevalent today. Despite thick fog these ships were both travelling at around 12 knots and that seems very fast in a busy river. The two pilots were in communication over VHF and they had each other on their radars as they closed in with a combined speed of 23 knots. This was an amazing collision as the ships crashed head on. Usually ships in this situation would glance off each other, but these two collided exactly bow to bow. One of the ships was penetrated right through, past the collision bulkhead and causing extensive damage, which eventually led to it partially sinking. The use of a mobile phone on the bridge was cited as a part of the cause of this collision; as with driving a car, they can be a considerable distraction. Nevertheless, travelling at high speed in fog was probably the major contributory cause.

Fog no longer seems to be a reason for slowing down. When I made a voyage down the River Rhine in 2006 in thick fog, it was quite frightening to see the big barges loaded with everything from liquid gas to containers maintaining full speed within the narrow confines of the river. Our river pilot said that there would be at least one collision on the river every day in foggy conditions and, sure enough, one occurred during our voyage, but fortunately we were not involved. Modern specialised river radars do allow other vessels to be detected within the confines of the river and if everyone adheres to the right lane discipline, collisions should not happen. Unfortunately, pressure is added when one vessel is overtaking another, and when vessels want to travel on the opposite side of the river to cheat the current.

The dangerous confines of rivers and harbours

River traffic will always seem high risk, even in clear weather. As always, there are the human errors that can lead to disaster. A captain travelling up a river in the United States put the position of a lighthouse in his chart plotter as a waypoint. He was rather surprised when the ship went aground right under it. It is tempting to use GPS positions on an electronic chart to plot positions when entering harbour, particularly when the visibility is poor. It will probably work most of the time, but the accuracy of normal GPS is only around 30m and that may not be enough to keep you in the deeper water of a narrow channel. If you get the plot wrong within the confines of a harbour the consequences can be more immediate and more serious.

The collision between the pleasure boat *Marchioness* and the 1,400 tonne dredger *Bowbelle* on the River Thames was a terrible tragedy. The *Marchioness* was taking a party of people out on the river for a celebration cruise at night, while the *Bowbelle* was heading downstream after discharging her cargo of sand. At 01:00, right in the middle of London, the dredger literally ran over the pleasure boat in the dark. Of the 131 people on board the *Marchioness*, 51 died.

It was established that the captain of the *Bowbelle* had drunk six pints of beer before sailing, but he was cleared of failing to keep a proper lookout. This accident led to considerable changes in marine safety. One of these changes demanded that pleasure boats on the Thames have a view astern from the wheelhouse, something that should be part of the basic design of any boat. A view astern from the helm is not a priority in the design of motor yachts today, and the design of many ships' bridges can be just as bad. Restricted visibility from the helm could easily lead you to miss important marks or other vessels, and this can often be the case when there is no view astern and a ship is overtaking.

An examination of the operation of pleasure-boats in harbours around the world reveals many accidents waiting to happen. Many of these boats will pack large numbers of passengers into a relatively small space, and because they tend to sail only in the apparently benign waters of harbours, this is not considered to be a major safety problem. One such boat, the *Al Dana*, capsized when it went to sea with 130 people on board. It was later revealed that it was licensed only as a floating restaurant and not for

The pleasure boat **Marchioness.**

sea-going trips. The *Al Dana* was also only licensed to carry 100 people and so went out in an overloaded condition. It appears that the crew made desperate pleas for the passengers not to crowd to one side just before the capsize.

Not before time, the rules regarding the design and operation of these so-called pleasure boats are being tightened up, but I am not sure that rules and regulations alone can do the job. As always with shipping and boating disasters, it is the human element that is the weak point. The best-designed and regulated boats in the world will not prevent disasters if the operating crew are not up to the job. There is always a feeling of shock and horror when these major disasters occur, but many cases are all too predictable. The trouble is that, more often than not, no one will take any notice of the dangers until after the event.

Damage to bridges

Colliding with bridges seems to be almost a national sport in the United States. There has been a wonderful video doing the rounds on the Internet, showing a ship steaming up a river in the Southern States. Someone clearly did not do their sums properly when measuring the clearance under a bridge. The bridge of the ship just made it but the funnel didn't; the ship was effectively decapitated. An inland tug did much the same thing when a river was in flood and the clearance was considerably reduced. Seeing the danger the tug captain tried to turn, but the current pushed him inexorably toward the bridge. The tug was turned on its side, scraped under the bridge and popped up on the other side. As the video caption stated, that is one way to wash down the decks.

A construction barge heading down a river (also in the United States) forgot to lower the jib of the crane on board, causing a nasty mess as the crane was toppled. A legal mess can also result from some of these bridge collisions. In one case the bridge was found to be at fault because the bridge keeper had not opened it in time. Much more serious was when a ship collided with one of the pillars of the huge suspension bridge that crosses the entrance channel to Tampa in Florida. The collision, with the SS *Summit Venture*, happened in a storm and caused 1,200ft of the road to plunge into the water, killing 35 people who were in trucks and buses on the road at the time. One car landed on the deck of the *Summit Venture* and the driver survived. If there is something solid in a river or harbour, then sooner or later a ship or boat will collide with it.

This large container ship hit one of the bridge piers at Oakland Harbour when trying to leave port in thick fog in order to keep to schedule.

One of the more recent bridge collisions occurred in the Port of Oakland when a container ship was leaving harbour in thick fog. The pilot who was conning the ship claimed that the radar gave him misleading information and he could not see the Racon that marked the centre of the passage span of the Oakland–San Francisco Bridge. He also claimed he could not see the buoys marking the passage or the bridge piers on the radar. The ship collided with one of those piers, creating a huge gash in the side of the ship and leaking 200 tonnes of fuel. Despite the protestations of the pilot, the radar was found to be in sound working order when checked later by investigators. You could ask why this large ship was negotiating a busy harbour in thick fog but this accident shows how ships take risks when they have to keep to tight schedules.

In 2002 a tugboat towing a barge laden with redundant subway cars collided with a railroad bridge over the Harlem River. Apparently the swing bridge was partly open at the time, and because of the damage could not be closed again. This caused serious delays to the railroad schedules but the tug, barge and subway cars survived. More recently an 800ft tanker collided with the I-10 Bridge at Baton Rouge on the Mississippi River. Damage was limited to the protective barriers installed to prevent bridge damage, so something was working as it should.

Putting a barrier across the Thames that could be closed to prevent flooding was asking for trouble, and it came in 1997 when the sand dredger *Sand Kite* was heading upriver. The 98m ship was loaded with 3,300 tonnes of sand and she collided with one of the concrete piers of the barrier as she attempted to pass through in thick fog. This holed the ship and she backed off. She then attempted to pass through another gap in the barrier, only for the bow to sink and effectively block the barrier. The ship was refloated after the cargo had been discharged and both the master of the ship and the authorities were blamed for the accident.

Bridges and jetties are not the only things to suffer at the hands of erratic ships. The minimum control of some of the inland shipping barges that operate on the rivers in the US when pushed by powerful tugs is demonstrated by the frequency with which they hit other ships as well as the fixtures. One of these big tows hit a casino ship on the Mississippi. There have been numerous cases of tows, which can measure up to a quarter-mile long, breaking apart and causing mayhem on the river. Favourite targets are the locks and dams that are used to control the water depths in the upper reaches of the river, and it is not unknown for barges to end up across the dams.

Hurricanes in harbours

Harbours are not called havens for nothing, but there are many places that are vulnerable in strong winds or with wind from a certain direction. The havoc that can be caused by hurricanes in marinas confirms that shelter is relative when the wind is this strong. Combine the strong winds with the tidal surge that is often associated with hurricanes and you have a recipe for disaster.

I have been through two hurricanes in my career: one in harbour, and one out at sea. Given the choice, I would prefer to ride out the storm at sea. We were in a port on the south coast of Cuba finishing off discharging when the hurricane was forecast. We would not have been able to get far enough out to sea to be safe, and the rickety wooden jetty that we were tied up to did not look as though it would survive the storm. The only viable solution was to flood all the ballast tanks and the empty cargo holds and sit the ship on the seabed. If nothing else this would take any strain off the mooring ropes, which would almost certainly have parted even if the jetty had held firm. It worked and we survived unscathed, but it was lethal outside, with sheets of corrugated iron whistling around in the wind threatening to decapitate anyone foolish enough to venture out.

A recent storm in a Black Sea harbour was responsible for the loss of 35 lives and for six vessels being washed ashore, with considerable pollution resulting from the spilt oil. This shows the vulnerability of some harbours and anchorages in strong winds. There are few parts of the world that are not exposed to

113

Marinas may not be the safest place to be in a hurricane.

storms of one kind or another, and many port builders take calculated risks about the level of protection they offer because it is too expensive to cover every storm eventuality. It is the same with marinas; many of them are built in marginal conditions where a swell coming into the harbour can spell disaster for the boats inside.

Not safe on land

The assumption is often that when a ship or boat is in the hands of repairers or out of the water, it is removed from danger. However, when a boat is out of its natural element, it can be more prone to damage than when it is in the water. One of the most awful moments of my life was when I was participating in the 1984 Round Britain Powerboat Race. We were winning this staged race by miles, and only had to complete the last leg from Ramsgate to Portsmouth to clinch the win. As was the practice at each overnight stop, the boat was craned out to check the propellers and underwater parts. Once swung over the quay, the crane driver extended the jib out to land the boat but it proved too much for the crane. The crane tipped and the boat – which was only half over the quay edge – dropped down and started to slide towards the 20ft drop back to the water. The situation was only saved when a big iron bollard on the quay pierced the bottom of the boat. This locked the boat in position, and the crane, relieved of its load, came back upright. But my heart was beating a lot faster because I was on the boat, and if it had dropped I think I would have faced certain death. Amazingly, we were able to repair the hole in the bottom under the engine beds by working overnight, and we went on to win the final leg and the race overall the following day.

One 56ft yacht took an unexpected nose dive when one of the lifting strops around the boat broke as the yacht was being discharged from a ship. As is so often the case, someone was on hand to take a photo of the event (see page 97) as the power yacht plunged vertically into the water. Amazingly the two people on board the yacht survived without harm, and this nose dive at least demonstrated how strong modern boats are.

114

A big Sunseeker was not so lucky when the yacht proved too heavy for the crane that was used to discharge it from a ship. Like our escapade in Ramsgate, the crane collapsed across the yacht causing severe damage.

Ship repair and building yards are dangerous places from all accounts. A floating dry dock sank under a large fishing boat after the weight of the boat proved too much for the deck of the dock, forcing the keel blocks through the plating. To add to the mess, the fishing boat capsized as the dock sank. One of the largest and most modern fishing boats in the Dutch fleet caught fire when undergoing a refit in a shipyard and became a total loss. The refit on the 142m vessel was almost complete when the fire started, and the vessel was in danger of capsizing because of the large amount of firefighting water being pumped on board. Another fishing vessel, the 78m *Atlantic Seahunter,* sank when she was being towed to a dry dock for her final fitting out. No cause has been given for the sinking, but it sounds like a case of an opening not being sealed off properly, letting water into the hull.

This large Sunseeker motor yacht suffered severe damage when the crane lifting it was not man enough for the job and collapsed over the boat.

During the war, the transatlantic liner *Normandie* caught fire in New York Harbour when she was being converted into a troop ship. Sparks from some welding work were thought to be the initial cause of the fire. She was totally burnt out, and because of the amount of water that was pumped on board to put out the fire she capsized. She was eventually salvaged, only to be scrapped.

A haven of peace and tranquillity?

This list of major disasters to ships in harbour can be matched by disasters to yachts and small craft. These may not be quite so dramatic but for the people involved they are certainly traumatic. People falling overboard, people getting run over by boats, boats in collision and boats sinking. Every harbour has its tale to tell, and I see the results of some of these accidents during the expert witness work that I do. Some of the worst are the people who go overboard and end up being injured by the boat's propeller. It seems to happen with surprising regularity. But drowning is still the number one cause of death in boating accidents. It is horrific that there have been close to 800 boating fatalities in the United States in one year, with many of them occurring in harbour and river waters.

Harbours should be a haven of peace and tranquillity at the end of a voyage, but just getting into the harbour can be a challenging task. Harbours with shallow water across the entrance can be dangerous when there is an onshore wind and an ebb tide running out. The breaking seas generated by these conditions can lead to boats broaching and capsizing just at the point when the thought of being home and dry is uppermost in your mind. Bar conditions can be the most challenging that many small boats face, and even lifeboats have come unstuck trying to enter harbour in severe conditions. One of the problems is that when coming in, it is not always possible to see how dangerous the waves are until you meet them, because the heavy breaking seas do not show up from seaward.

115

We had some indication of the danger we were facing when entering St Augustine harbour on passage down the Florida coast. This was a planned refuelling stop so we were getting low on fuel. We had spent the night cruising down the coast running at 35 knots in the low swell coming in from the Atlantic. Then we entered the fog around the harbour entrance and that lazy swell was now running heavy and white as it encountered the shallows. Suddenly this leisurely cruise had reached critical mass, with the big breaking seas in the entrance channel, the fog limiting our ability to see the buoys marking the channel and the low fuel, which meant that we had little alternative but to go for the entrance.

'Here, you're the expert (I had written a book about driving boats in rough seas), you take over,' said the skipper, 'I'll look out for the channel buoys.' Finding these buoys was critical as there was a dog-leg in the entrance and if we missed that we could end up aground in the breaking seas. We ran into that entrance from the fairway buoy with the big breaking waves curling up behind us. I was watching astern rather than ahead to make sure we could accelerate away from any breaking wave that was catching up and luckily the buoys came up out of the fog on schedule. It was a critical time and if we made one mistake we would probably end up dead. This was riding the knife edge, but it worked and there was a considerable sense of relief when we tied up for fuel. Our mistake was to let the fuel get low at a critical time, and this episode clearly demonstrated how a situation can escalate into near disaster in harbour entrances at the end of a voyage.

No place to relax

I can't help feeling that it is a harbour's very image of safety and security that accounts for some of the disasters that happen there. You start to relax even before you enter the harbour, convinced that you are now home and dry, the voyage has ended and it is downhill from now on. I have seen it happen on several occasions. The bottle comes out as soon as the sea becomes calm in the confines of a harbour. The skipper and crew start to relax and unwind, forgetting that there is still what can be the most difficult part of the voyage ahead. Coming into a harbour at night can be one of the most challenging experiences for any navigator.

It can be equally difficult when leaving harbour. You just want to fire up the engines and go, forgetting that you should be going through all the preparation sequences before you leave the berth. I have done it myself and found I needed to get the right display on the electronic chart, get the radar set up and try to find the right course to follow once clear of the harbour. It is easy to preach but I do like to try to keep at the back of my mind the navy phrase, 'Being in all respects ready for sea'. I doubt whether many of us, professionals and amateurs alike, could put our hands on our hearts and say that we did all the preparation work necessary before heading out. It is possible to get away with it once out in the open seas, but in harbours and their approaches time is not on your side and quick assessments and decisions are needed. Yachtsmen can have the advantage here because they will usually be familiar with their boats and equipment. The big ship crews may only have joined their new ship a few hours before and could be struggling to understand the new equipment and systems at this critical time. They could be classed as being 'In all respects not ready for sea'.

Harbours are dangerous places where the calm waters lull you into a false sense of security. You don't wear lifejackets, you don't take precautions and despite the crowded waters your approach to boating is more relaxed. That is the time the sea catches you out and you become extremely vulnerable.

MARINE ACCIDENT INVESTIGATION BRANCH

Overtaking in a harbour entrance

Narrative

A yacht engaged in RYA training of four student skippers was entering harbour, and had lined up to pass a particularly narrow part of the channel. An experienced yachtmaster instructor was in overall charge, and all five crew were on deck. The sails had been furled and the engine was running. Everything was normal.

As the yacht was making its approach, the skipper noticed that a fishing boat was overtaking them from astern, and instructed the helmsman to maintain course and speed. He fully expected the fisherman to slow down because he thought it was obvious there was insufficient room for both vessels to pass through the very narrow gap ahead at the same time.

He was wrong. The fishing boat increased speed to overtake to port. When it was abeam and only 2m off, it became clear that a dangerous situation was developing, with insufficient room for both vessels to fit through the gap. The yacht now found itself severely hampered because any turn to starboard would have resulted in her port quarter hitting the overtaking fishing vessel. The only option available was to take all way off by applying full astern power. She did so.

The fishing vessel completed her overtaking manoeuvre, but not before her starboard quarter had given the yacht's port bow a glancing blow with, fortunately, only minor damage.

In the verbal exchange that followed, the fishing vessel skipper said that because he was working, yachts should keep out of his way, and that the yacht should have used another channel.

No damage was done, but the incident left the five yachtsmen very shaken.

The Lessons

1

From whatever the perspective, this relatively minor accident should not have happened, but the lessons must be learned before something much more serious occurs.

2

If you are the skipper of a small vessel entering a harbour, you may well encounter another small craft ahead of you doing likewise. Unless Rule of the Road No. 9 applies ('A vessel of less than 20m in length or a sailing vessel shall not impede the passage of a vessel which can safely navigate only within a narrow channel or fairway'), or there is some bylaw that states otherwise, the overtaking vessel is bound to 'keep out of the way of the vessel being overtaken'. Most often this means the overtaking vessel should slow down.

3

A fishing vessel is indeed a 'working' vessel, but when not engaged in fishing she is just like any other, and must follow the 'Rules' as such.

4

If approaching a very narrow channel or gap, and going faster than the vessel ahead, give thought to the consequences of trying to overtake. It is good seamanship to anticipate the room required for manoeuvring, any shallow water effect, and the possibility of an outbound vessel affecting your ability to alter course or even the likelihood of interaction between the two craft. The obvious solution in practically every case is to slow down and wait for a more opportune moment to overtake. Patience is everything.

5

Remember that if the craft being overtaken is a yacht and you are likely to pass very close, she may well pivot around her keel if required to alter course. If she does so, her stern will swing out in the opposite direction to the turn.

6

Overtaking another craft to leave no more than 2m between you in circumstances such as those described is neither clever nor sensible. Put more bluntly, it is dangerous.

7

Skippers should always be prepared for the person overtaking to do something unseamanlike – or stupid. Or put the other way round, the man being overtaken may equally do something pretty silly in front of you. Expect the unexpected.

Rescues

It might sound odd, but you are not rescued until safely on dry land. The focus of a rescue is always on getting the passengers and crew off the ship that is in trouble. That is what lifeboats and liferafts are all about, but that is only half the rescue story. There are horror stories of people getting away from sinking ships, only to be lost when someone tries to pick them up. Rescue at sea can be a torturous, dangerous process and you can never be certain that you aren't leaping from the frying pan into the fire during the rescue process. Dry land never looks so appealing as when seen after a rescue.

A rescue swimmer comes to the aid of a lady survivor whose boat is sinking under her.

Don't leave the boat

Victims of disaster are probably already in a state of shock by the time rescue arrives. The ship or small craft may have suffered grounding, collision, fire or some combination of disasters that means it is time to leave. Simply knowing when to do so is a major decision; all the textbooks insist you should not leave your vessel unless it is actually sinking beneath you. It is best to wait for the very last opportunity because liferafts are not an appealing option. The sense of relief at getting away from a sinking ship is soon tempered by the fragility of the liferaft. I can tell you from personal experience that a liferaft feels very lonely and vulnerable in the middle of a vast ocean, and at that point in time you are barely halfway to being rescued.

Who should decide?

There is a tendency in any rescue situation to let those attempting the rescue take charge. In many cases the rescuers, such as lifeboat crews, will be the best men for the job, but any non-professional rescuer will be just as nervous about what to do and what is going to happen as the person sitting in the liferaft. The whole experience will be new to both the victim and the rescue crew, for whom every rescue is different, even if they are experts in their field. The rescuers prefer to take charge and dictate the terms of the procedure and, desperate for a resolution, the survivor will usually acquiesce. However, in my experience, it doesn't hurt to have an input into how the rescue is going to be effected because after all, you are the person in the firing line.

Rescue by a big ship

I nearly died when a big ship tried to rescue me and the crew from the sinking *Chaffeteaux Challenger*. While we were at fault for needing rescue, there were many lessons to be learnt for us all. *Chaffeteaux Challenger* was an 80ft sailing catamaran in which we were trying to set a new Atlantic sailing record. It was April in the North Atlantic, a great time for strong winds but also very cold and uncomfortable. We had got out of sync with the weather patterns that were supposed to speed us across the Atlantic and instead hit storm after storm with winds of over 100 knots at times. We were delayed too much to have any hope of the record and had switched into semi-survival mode just to finish the Atlantic crossing. That was when we saw cracks starting to appear in the hull around the open cockpit area.

The cracks continued to grow and one evening we held a council of war. Another storm was coming in and we decided it was time to call for help. We felt the risks of being rescued at night were too great and decided to wait till dawn. I called the Coastguard to let them know our predicament and we arranged to call every hour, on the hour, with an updated position. If we failed to make one of those hourly calls then the Coastguard would initiate a search as the likelihood would be that our boat had finally broken in two.

I could feel the tension as I made these regular calls and the relief at the other end when we made contact. It was a long night. The Coastguard arranged for a rescue ship to rendezvous with us at daylight.

Come the dawn there was this huge container ship steaming to the rescue. With a length of 900ft and 40ft from the water to the deck this ship was far from ideal, but beggars cannot be choosers. We watched with trepidation as the ship came alongside us, its bow rising and falling in the waves, seemingly just feet away. The captain did a brilliant job in parking the ship alongside and we looked up to see a crewman on deck. 'Throw us a rope,' we cried, only to hear the response, 'We don't have any ropes on this ship.'

A huge container vessel is far from being the ideal rescue ship. Out in the ocean you are not in a position to choose but it would help if such ships were prepared for this type of operation.

Unable to secure the boat we drifted aft, scraping along the ship's side until the rigging caught in a projection. The mast came down, but fortunately we all escaped injury from the ton of falling metal.

Worse was to follow. Without the mast the boat came to the stern and was sucked into the propeller's space. We saw the 28ft diameter propeller turning ever so slowly, and then it started to

121

*Alongside the rescue ship in Chaffeteaux Challenger, **but you are not rescued until you are safe on deck.***

chop bits off our bow like a big bacon slicer. It was like a scene from a James Bond film, except if this got worse we were going to die. And then it did get worse. Once we were right under the stern of the ship it came down on top of us. I was in the cross beam of the catamaran where the headroom should have been 4ft, but with the weight of the ship, it was now squashed to merely 2ft and we were underwater. The situation was now completely out of control, but amazingly the boat popped out of the stern when the ship lifted. After a real struggle, I managed to crawl out of the cross beam hatch to find that none of our seven-man crew had suffered even a scratch. This was remarkable considering our predicament, but we still had not been rescued and were now scared stiff of getting anywhere near the ship.

We then did what we should have done earlier, and had a long discussion with the captain about how to proceed on the second attempt. This time they found a rope to secure us alongside and all went well. There was even a powered pilot hoist to take us up the ship's side in our exhausted and emotional state. We felt a great sense of relief in standing on the deck of the ship still in one piece. We then encountered true American hospitality by being asked to sign a disclaimer that we would not sue them because they had damaged our boat!

Our experience demonstrates two key principles. Firstly, that sending the nearest ship is not always the best solution. If a smaller ship had been sent, it would probably have been easier and safer. Secondly, if there is time, the rescue attempt should always be discussed before an attempt is made. Just getting alongside is the easy part: holding the boat there and getting up the ship's side is the hard bit. Ultimately, we were of course very grateful indeed to be rescued and still be alive.

It was a close call and it made me realise that the margins between success and failure in these situations can be very small. I like to think that if we had discussed how the rescue was to take place before it commenced, then we might have suggested that they have a rope ready when we came alongside the ship. Another lesson learned was that most ships are not equipped to carry out rescue work. There seems to be a feeling among the Coastguard that if they send a ship to the rescue then it is 'job done', and the hard work is left to the ship. The captain of the *Sealand Performance* was not willing to risk his crew by lowering a lifeboat to come and take us off, and I can't say I blame him. The lifeboat on that ship was located too close to the propeller for comfort. It is important to appreciate that ships' crews have little or no experience in launching and recovering boats at sea and even less experience in handling them. I am always amazed that ships do manage to carry out rescues in bad weather, despite their lack of experience, and it reflects enormous credit on the crew's skill and seamanship. Just parking that huge container ship alongside us in rough seas and strong winds was a lesson in consummate seamanship, but I do wish he had stopped his propeller.

The final lesson learned from that rescue was when to call for help. I think we did the right thing by calling in early. Just placing that call does not guarantee help will be sent straight away. Of course there are situations where immediate help will be needed, but when a deteriorating situation on board becomes apparent, then it is best to let the Coastguard know right away. An early warning call can enable rescue plans to be set up, but the decision on whether or not to put them into action remains yours. That night we had a strong motive for informing the Coastguard of our dire situation as it could have deteriorated rapidly, leaving us without the ability to send a further call for help. Equally, we were concerned that rescue at night, when everything is that much more difficult, could have had dire consequences. Every rescue situation is different and logical thought is not always easy, but it is best to have some sort of plan rather than rush into a rescue. That applies to both the rescued and the rescuer.

Deciding when to leave

When in trouble, a yachtsman faces the dilemma of whether to stay aboard or leave his vessel. In a very serious situation, such as a fire, there may not be a choice, but often there are options. Deciding on the right time to leave is very difficult; once you have departed there will be little or no chance of going back. The perceived wisdom is that you should stay with your boat for as long as possible because boats can survive a lot longer than one might expect and will be easier for any searchers to find. Jump into the liferaft and you could find yourself heading rapidly downwind in a strong blow, away from the position you reported. A liferaft is a very fragile craft with little or no means for control. While the raft might feel quite large to you once inside, it is a tiny speck in a vast ocean for any searchers. These rafts are also prone to capsize in rough seas, which can seriously reduce the chances of survival. Think very carefully about using a liferaft if close to a lee shore unless it offers a sandy beach landing. Liferafts are offered as the panacea to all disasters, but in my experience they should only be used as a last resort.

Take the case of Tony Bullimore, when his yacht lost its keel in the Southern Ocean. He probably did not have the option of abandoning his boat after it capsized, and must have been thankful for the survival suit he was wearing in those extreme conditions. The point is that the boat was found because his EPIRB was beeping away and even though it took three days to reach the spot, he was rescued. It could have been a very different story if he had abandoned the yacht and taken to his liferaft.

This rescue and many others emphasise how important communications are in a disaster. Help cannot be sent if no one knows you are in trouble, so when planning your safety equipment put communications at the top of the list. It is such a boost to morale to be able to talk to someone from your position in the liferaft. A waterproof, hand-held radio is the best safety device ever invented in my book, with an EPIRB coming a close second.

EPIRBs

EPIRBs have transformed rescue work because they can indicate a vessel is in trouble and give the rescuers a position. In the days before electronics took over, it was a matter of luck whether another ship came along to the rescue. The *Titanic* was one of the first ships to send out a radio distress message. Today it is best to have an EPIRB to send out a distress call, even from the liferaft, and a portable VHF to talk to the rescuers; this will make time spent in a raft a much more positive experience. With just an EPIRB the distress message is sent out, but you have no idea if it has been received, and if it has, what action is being taken to rescue you.

EPIRBs have done a great job in making it more practical for vessels to call for help but they have also greatly increased the problem of false alarms. It is reckoned that something like 90% of distress messages sent out by EPIRBs are false alarms, and these can take up a lot of the emergency services' time. Coastguards tend to look quite carefully at distress messages received from EPIRBs but they cannot afford to take chances and so must send out lifeboats or helicopters just in case. I have to confess to being responsible for one such false alarm when I was safe in harbour. We were completing a Round Britain Powerboat Race and had arrived safely in Dundee. A rescue helicopter descended out of the sky having pinpointed a distress signal from an EPIRB. It was with considerable embarrassment that I discovered it was our EPIRB sending out the signal. We had not switched it on, but it must have been set off by the pounding of the boat when out at sea. The helicopter crew were not best pleased. Another incident had an EPIRB signal reported off Belfast. The lifeboat went out to investigate and found the signal coming from the shore. Further investigation showed that the signal was coming from a rubbish tip on shore where an EPIRB had been discarded. The future should bring an EPIRB that allows voice communication, and then these false alarms can be reduced.

Electronics and water

There are many people who will argue that it is folly to rely on electronics at sea, citing the inevitable unreliability of electronics when mixed with water. However, when it comes to rescue work, electronics have a major role to play. A case in point comes from the experience of veteran sailor Michael Richey, who was sailing the famous *Jester* back across the Atlantic after competing in the single-handed transatlantic race. The boat was knocked down in a severe storm and Michael badly injured his back. Almost unable to move, he managed to activate the EPIRB. Help arrived in the form of the *Geest Bay* and he was rescued. Amazingly it was the *Geest Bay* that had rescued us from *Virgin Atlantic Challenger* just a year earlier, within a few miles of the same location and on almost the same date. Without electronics, Michael might not have survived.

Looking back at the Fastnet disaster of 1979 it is easy to see how things could have been better organised with superior communications. So often a sailboat will lose its radio when the mast comes down and the antenna is gone. I have little faith in the traditional remedy of flares and smoke to attract attention. Even with the limited range of a hand-held VHF radio, the ability to inform people of your location and situation is a vital step toward being rescued. When reading accounts of that Fastnet disaster it is possible to imagine the loneliness of the crews out there, stuck in a rapidly deteriorating situation out of their control and without means of communication.

Richard Branson and Chay Blyth in the liferaft from Virgin Atlantic Challenger **with the first aircraft on the scene seen in the background. From that point we knew that help was close.**

Taking to the liferaft

We did not have a choice about taking to the liferaft when our beloved *Virgin Atlantic Challenger* was sinking. After the hull split open, we knew that the boat was going to sink and we had to get off. We probably knew before that point, because it was going down by the stern quite rapidly. It was the heavy weight of the engines that were taking the stern down and as there were no waterproof bulkheads in the boat the water automatically ran to that point. As this was a high-risk venture we had practised the art of abandoning ship before we left, so we all had assigned tasks and knew precisely what to do. My task was to get on the radio and let someone know that we were in trouble. I tried on the HF radio but could not get any response to our relatively weak signal. Then I tried on the VHF, hoping that there were some ships close by that might pick up our distress message.

We were close to the busy shipping lanes in the Western Approaches, but there was no reply and worry set in. I had also triggered the Argos location beacon, a specialized unit something like an EPIRB that had an automatic distress mode that would give out our position, although there could be some delay in the message being received. By the time I had done this, the water was coming up my legs and it was time to get out. The water was also up over the batteries and the radios were not working. The crew had got the liferafts in the water and loaded useful stores, such as a case of gin and tonics. We climbed on board and remained tied on to *Challenger* for a while before cutting loose, fearing that we might get taken down with the boat when it went.

Watching your boat die

As we drifted away, the two liferafts tied together so that we stayed in contact, we watched our boat getting lower and lower in the water until just the bow was showing above the waves. We had spent so much time with that boat that it was like watching an old friend die, but of greater concern was whether anyone would come to our rescue. It was late in the afternoon and we faced the prospect of a long, lonely night in the wild waters of the Atlantic. Then we saw an aircraft flying low overhead and knew that help would be on its way. As it happened this aircraft was not a response to our distress messages, but simply a press aeroplane that had flown out to get some photographs of the boat powering its way to the finish line and a new Atlantic record. They ended up with a much better story than expected.

Now it was starting to get dark – it is hard to comprehend just how lonely it feels out on the huge ocean in a tiny liferaft. The prospect of a long night in the raft was not something I wanted to contemplate, but where were the rescue ships? They would struggle to find us in the dark and some of our crew were already deteriorating through seasickness. I had had the forethought to take a seasick pill before abandoning ship, knowing how the motion of a liferaft can make even the most immune of sailors seasick. Sickness does not make for a pleasant liferaft. Everyone wanted to be

I took this photo of the sinking Virgin Atlantic Challenger *as I was sitting in the liferaft awaiting rescue.*

beside the two small openings in the cover to get fresh air, so we had to establish a rota. We were lucky to have only five people in a ten-man liferaft. Had the full complement been on board, I dread to think what it would have been like inside.

Finally, after what seemed like an eternity but in reality was little over an hour, a ship was seen approaching. Our distress messages had been heard and here was a ship coming to the rescue. It was the *Geest Bay*, a banana ship out of Barry on its way to the Caribbean for another load of bananas. The wind was blowing about Force 6 and the captain did a superb job of parking his big ship alongside our tiny liferafts, making the final connection by firing a rocket line over us. Once we were pulled alongside, the gangway was lowered and as there were no women or children on board I felt no guilt about getting out first and climbing that gangway to the security of the ship's deck. There, at the top of the gangway, was a steward in a white jacket and a black bow tie with a silver tray holding glasses of brandy. 'Would you like a drink, sir?' What a welcome back to the real world; neatly emphasising the difference between rescue by a British ship and the lawyer's welcome we received when rescued from *Chaffeteaux Challenger* by the American ship.

We had been in our own little world for the previous three days, shut up in the wheelhouse of a fast boat trying to cross the Atlantic. We had no idea of the impact we were having on the outside world. Apparently we were the lead item on the 6 o'clock news that evening, announcing we were on schedule to break the record. The news ended by saying that our distress call had been received, and then the country sat on the edge of its seat waiting for more news. It was only afterwards that we could understand why both the Air Force and the Navy sent out helicopters to take us ashore. I think the captain of the *Geest Bay* was really disappointed that we would not stay to dinner with his passengers.

The crew of Chaffeteaux Challenger *on the bridge of the rescue ship* Sealand Performance.

AMVER

Being rescued by a passing ship is as much as can be expected in the middle of the ocean, when out of the range of shore-based rescue. I am full of admiration for the way that ordinary ships manage to effect a rescue, and many of them are members of a voluntary system called AMVER that tracks ships across the oceans. This system allows the Coastguard to pinpoint the nearest ship to an incident, enabling the mutual support system whereby ships and boats help each other when in trouble. It is one of the great traditions of the sea that ships willingly go to the rescue of others, even in today's tough commercial climate.

This support system can also work when there is a medical emergency on board. Most passenger ships are required to carry a doctor, which is looked on as something of a cushy job. However, the doctor really earns his keep when he has to be transferred to another ship in the middle of the ocean. Even passenger ships with their rigid inflatable rescue boats are not really equipped for transfers at sea. This is mainly because the crews have very little experience of launching the rescue boat and recovering it from its stowage on a high-sided ship in rough seas. It is about time that the business of launching and recovering boats from ships is reviewed and that a better and safer way of doing things is found.

A boat in distress will be in much better hands close to land, due to the proximity of both lifeboats and helicopters with professionals available to do the job. Increasingly all rescue work is left to these services, even though there may be other boats in the vicinity. There seems to be a growing reluctance for yachts, both power and sail, to get involved in an actual rescue. They would rather inform the Coastguard and then simply stand by. Given the limited rescue experience of most sailors and the risk of damage to their vessels, this reluctance is understandable. I like to think that in the event of a dire emergency they would go in and do the job. Perhaps this action would be encouraged if the insurance companies indicated that they would pick up the bill for any resulting damage. At present, the question of who pays for damage sustained in a rescue is something of a grey area.

Helicopter rescue

Helicopters have transformed rescue work and they do a very impressive job. Even 40 years ago, when I was working with lifeboats, it was often the helicopter that was first on the scene and effected the rescue. Their ability to pluck people from small craft is quite amazing and I am always impressed when I see them operating close in to towering cliffs and similarly dangerous areas. Some helicopters send a crewman down on the hoist wire to help get the survivors into the strop and away to safety. That was the system used after we were taken off our liferaft by the *Geest Bay*. Others send down a rescue basket into which the survivors must climb. It is very reassuring to have one of the helicopter crew come down on the wire, someone professional taking control of the situation, ensuring all goes smoothly.

Modern helicopters can operate at night, although this does increase the risks as it is not so easy to judge distances. Modern helicopters can also operate a long way out to sea, usually to distances of over 100 miles, and can be a very effective solution to many medical emergencies. Helicopters and lifeboats appear to work in close harmony in Europe, where they tend to be operated by two separate organisations, while in the US it is the Coastguard who operates both helicopters and lifeboats. The merits of whether lifeboats should be a full-time service funded by government or a voluntary organisation supported by public contributions is open to discussion. Both systems seem to work well and it is easy to see the reluctance of governments to take over the funding when the service is effective without interference.

I know from first hand experience the feeling of both nervousness and anticipation that comes with going out in a lifeboat to the rescue. The nervousness comes from having to cope with a situation that may only become clear once you arrive at the scene. There are no textbooks and no hard-and-fast rules when it comes to rescue work. You need both experience and initiative to sort things out as you go along. Get it wrong and someone could die, so the tension can be considerable. The sense of

The occupants of this sailing dinghy are trying to right the boat while a rescue boat stands by.

anticipation comes from the excitement of venturing into the unknown and facing the challenge. I found the same feeling when testing new designs of lifeboat, going out into very rough seas – that same nervousness of doubting one's ability to cope coupled with the excitement of having the chance to test one's capabilities to the full.

You are not safe yet

I recollect going out with a lifeboat to investigate a report of an upturned dinghy about two miles off the coast. It sounded a simple enough job and the reports stated that two people were clinging to the hull. When we arrived at the dingy, the 'two people' turned out to be the centreboard and the rudder sticking up from the upturned hull. So where had the crew gone to? A quick search of the immediate area showed nothing; now it was time to stop and think. It was obvious the crew had not stayed with the boat, and logic suggested they had set out to swim to the nearest shore. We made the line to the shore the priority search, and sure enough we found the sole occupant when he was just a couple of hundred yards from shore. Even if he had reached the shore he would have been in trouble, as it only comprised big boulders and steep cliffs. When we reached him he had become helpless in the water and close to drowning. By the time we had actually picked him up he was unconscious. This underscores the point that a victim is not rescued until safely on board the rescue vessel and preferably on dry land. It helps rescue crews a great deal if survivors can contribute to the rescue process.

Lifeboat rescues

There have been innumerable instances where the lifeboats have rescued crews from seemingly impossible situations. Most of these do seem to have occurred in the past, which makes me wonder if the days of heroic lifeboat rescues are over. In some respects, this could be due to the advances in the capabilities of the helicopter rescue services. These seem to deal with most of the more extreme rescues, when a ship or boat is on the rocks or sinking in severe weather. In the past, lifeboats would have had to cope and the records show some incredible rescues against the odds. I remember one rescue, when the lifeboat was alongside a ship and trying to take the crew off, when one of the ship's lifeboats fell on top of the rescue lifeboat. This is the sort of event that goes way beyond any experience developed from normal boating, and the lifeboat crews do an incredible job when faced with this sort of situation.

There have been times when the lifeboat crews themselves have been the ones in trouble. In severe weather no boat is fully immune to the stresses and challenges of the sea. Since its inception over 150 years ago, more than 450 RNLI lifeboat men have lost their lives when on active service. Among this appalling statistic are a surprising number of lifeboat disasters that occurred on the return to harbour. Fourteen crew were lost when the Rye Harbour lifeboat, on the south coast of England, was returning to harbour. I wonder how many of these disasters occur because crews begin to relax as they near home. Of course, crossing a dangerous bar at a harbour entrance is never going to be easy in a gale. This high-risk operation, when the drogue is put out and the boat has to negotiate the heavy breaking seas in the entrance, is fraught with danger. I have done it in a gale coming in over the Doom Bar at Padstow, and it was the drogue that made the difference between life and death.

So often in these situations, what actually happened is never fully known. The Fraserburgh lifeboat disaster off the east coast of Scotland, when all the crew were lost, shows how easily things can go wrong. Here the lifeboat had arrived at the scene of the casualty where other ships were already standing by. Initially all the lifeboat had to do was wait around and watch while a tug tried to take the casualty in tow. The lifeboat had had a stressful passage and on arrival the crew may have been relaxing when the boat was overtaken by a huge following sea and capsized. These days, with self-righting lifeboats, such an incident probably wouldn't happen. However, a self-righting boat is one thing but a self-righting crew is another. If they are to survive the experience then the crew must remain strapped into their seats at all times. The self-righting Penlee lifeboat *Solomon Browne* was lost, along with the crew of the ship (*Union Star*) that they were trying to rescue. This demonstrates that even with the best-built boats there is still a serious risk involved when trying to rescue others.

In the United States even their 44ft self-righting lifeboats are not immune from disaster. On a rescue in 1997, the Quillayute lifeboat was capsized three times in heavy seas, one of them a pitch-pole, and ended up being washed ashore with half its superstructure missing. Amazingly, one of the four-man crew survived the experience. However, American lifeboat tragedies appear less frequently than those found on exposed and rocky coastlines in Europe.

A dangerous game

Being rescued and doing the rescue work is a dangerous game. I can see why ships can be reluctant to risk their crews and go to the rescue of others in distress. Captains get no medals if their crew is injured or killed during a rescue operation, yet nobody has found a better solution for rescue in mid-ocean. Some countries, like the United States, have large cruising ships equipped with both helicopters and rescue boats that can come to the aid of vessels in distress, assuming they are within range. Other than that, it is fellow ships that must do the job established by the best traditions of the sea. By and large they do a good job, even if they do lack experience. However, most casualties occur much closer to the shore and probably 95% of them occur within range of lifeboats or helicopters containing professionals much better equipped for rescue work. With modern electronic communications providing vessels with the means to indicate that they are in trouble, and very capable helicopters and lifeboats available for rescue, the mariner has never been better provided with rescue facilities. I wonder how much this safety net encourages a more casual attitude towards safety and self-sufficiency at sea.

MARINE ACCIDENT INVESTIGATION BRANCH

Man overboard fatality from keelboat

Narrative

Two men and a woman, students at the UK Sailing Academy on the Isle of Wight, were sailing an Etchell 22 keelboat in the Solent. A 6m launch with two instructors on board was close by. It was May, the weather was good, the wind was force 3–4 and the water temperature was about + 11°C. All was well, until the Etchell gybed unintentionally and knocked one of the two men overboard. The man was properly dressed, wearing full sailing waterproofs with a fleece underneath and an ISON lifejacket. He was not injured when he fell overboard, but although he was fit and generally in good health, he weighed about 127kg (20 stone).

The attendant launch with the two instructors on board came to the immediate assistance of the man overboard for what was assumed to be a straightforward recovery. The launch had a freeboard of 0.8m, and to the dismay of the instructors, they found they could not lift him out. At first the man was able to assist his would-be rescuers, but he soon tired. After about 4 minutes he became unconscious, and very soon stopped breathing. The Coastguard and the sailing academy were informed about what had happened, as one of the instructors went into the water to begin mouth-to-mouth resuscitation on the casualty. A rescue helicopter was on the scene about 25 minutes later, and the casualty was airlifted to hospital on the Isle of Wight. However, despite continuous attempts to revive him, he was eventually pronounced dead. One of the academy's RIBs, which had responded to the emergency call, arrived five minutes after the helicopter.

The Lessons

1

This accident occurred despite every reasonable precaution being taken. The Sailing Academy had given much thought about how to prevent accidents, and how to react should one occur. The man was sensibly dressed for keelboat sailing, and was wearing a lifejacket. A launch was close by with two instructors on board who saw what had happened and were able to provide assistance within seconds of the man going overboard. And yet, despite all this, a man died. Anyone studying this accident will realise that one thing had been overlooked. Recovering anyone from the water is always much more difficult than almost anyone ever realises, but in this instance, trying to lift someone weighing 20 stone is very nearly impossible without the manpower, the lifting purchase, or sufficiently low freeboard to achieve it.

2

Cold shock, combined with the general trauma of having suffered a sudden accident, can occasionally cause death very quickly.

3

Losing a person overboard should always be considered a possibility whatever the craft being sailed, and whatever the weather conditions. There should be well-rehearsed routines, and specific equipment to aid the recovery of any of the boat's occupants, whatever their size or disability.

4

Crew members of very large stature, or crew members otherwise restricted in their mobility and agility, are particularly vulnerable, especially in a performance sailing craft with a low boom height. The particular risks should be thoroughly assessed before a voyage, and if necessary, extra precautions should be taken to cope with an emergency.

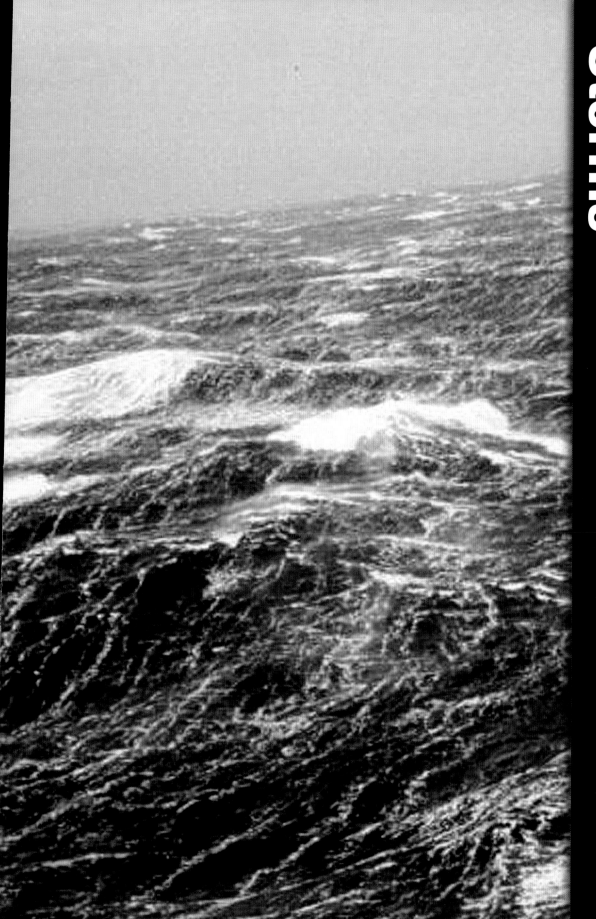

Storms

Storms

Astorm at sea is one of the most exhilarating experiences for a mariner, but it can also be one of the scariest. In a way, it is a shame that so few people get the chance to experience this, and even seamen are encouraged to stay in harbour when a storm rages. It is easy to take the safe option and not go to sea in a storm; in fact this is what all the textbooks advise, but out there in a storm, you ride the narrow line between success and failure. This is the ultimate thrill ride and is even more exciting than man-made efforts, because it lasts so much longer. Out in the storm it is your skills that decide whether you survive or not, and so represents a challenge that very little on earth can equal. You challenge nature in the raw, but the boat plays a big part too. If the boat fails, then the chances are you will fail as well.

Waiting for the storm

Does this sound crazy? Well, it probably is, but I have been lucky enough not only to go to sea in the wildest of storms, but to have a reason for doing so. For most seamen, a storm is something to be feared; something you encounter when the odds have been stacked against you and your only thought is to fight for survival. For me it was a question of waiting for the storm and then going out to sea.

I have to thank the RNLI for the chance to go to sea when the prudent seaman stays in harbour. My job was to test new designs of lifeboat and my brief was simple: 'Go out in the worst conditions you can find and see what happens.' This premeditated approach to experiencing storms provides a whole new

Few boatbuilders test their new designs in rough conditions, unlike this new pilot boat for Cork in Ireland.

angle to the problem. For most seamen the storm comes along because you have run out of luck and there is no way to avoid it. I too encountered storms in that way during five years roaming the world in a tramp ship. But lifeboat testing was a whole new experience and one I approached with a high degree of trepidation. One of the most positive factors was that I could be reasonably certain I had a sound boat beneath me that had been designed for the job. When you read accounts of sailors in storms, the downward cycle toward disaster usually starts with some sort of failure. Gear or machinery failure, no matter how simple, distracts a sailor's attention from the focus on survival, and that is of primary importance if he is to weather the storm.

I had no, or at least few, worries about the reliability of a lifeboat, and it is reliability that is the main difference between lifeboats and other small craft. Lifeboats are designed *not* to fail and that allows you to concentrate on the way the boat is performing and getting the job done. Most soundly constructed boats

A US lifeboat operating in very heavy breaking waves. Lifeboats are designed for this but other boats can be in serious trouble in these conditions.

with good equipment can weather a storm. A lifeboat not only has to weather the storm, but it must also have something left over to cope with the vessel in distress. It is a tall order and one that requires a strong focus on the detailed design of the boat.

It was exciting to push a boat beyond what you thought was reason and see what happened. That was the thrilling part of the job, to cope with the storm and analyse what was happening to the vessel. How did the boat behave in different wave patterns and conditions? How did handling of the boat vary in different conditions? Was there something left over that would enable the boat to carry out rescue work in the worst conditions? This testing gave me an insight into the performance of boats in fine weather and foul, a skill that few people have the chance to learn.

Taking seamanship to the limits in this way was exciting and one particular voyage stands out in my memory. It was a voyage from Rosslare in Ireland across the St George's Channel to Land's End and around to Falmouth. The boat was a new 48ft lifeboat design in the traditional mould, a double ender with a speed of only 9 knots, but designed to cope with anything the sea could throw at it. The boat had spent a couple of weeks out on the west coast of Ireland looking for Atlantic storms but had found little to test its capabilities. I joined the boat in Rosslare for the trip home and we promptly ran into exactly the sort of storm we'd been looking for: a force 10 from the north-west, running right down the Irish Sea, generating a huge following sea, the sort of conditions that can be a real challenge to a small boat. We set out in the late afternoon and were still in the shelter of land as we rounded the Kish Lighthouse for the run south. As we cleared land and the wind strengthened, conditions grew steadily worse. Soon we were among enormous breakers that reared up behind us and carried us forward in a great surge down the face of the wave like an express train. Once the wave crest had gone hissing past, the boat struggled at an uphill angle on the back of the wave until gradually the angle altered and we returned to the downhill rush again.

At a rough guess, I would say that those waves were close to 30ft high, possibly more, and I discovered why windows are put in the roof of the wheelhouse on lifeboats. Looking through those windows I had a clear view of the wave coming from behind and the breaking crest towering above us. It was awesome, but once we got into the rhythm of the waves I didn't want it to stop. Most of the crew were thoroughly seasick in the rough conditions, and I would normally have succumbed as well, but I suspect the excitement kept me going. I spent most of the night on the wheel and revelled in the performance of the boat. I thought about putting out the drogue to help stabilise the steering, but the boat performed so well it wasn't necessary.

It was a roller coaster ride all the way down the Irish Sea, and became even better when we picked up Land's End right on the nose, after a night at sea in storm conditions with cross tides. Call it luck or skill but that landfall was the icing on the cake of one of the most exciting nights of my life and the boat came through with flying colours.

I was on a high after that storm, and I don't think it was just relief at having survived. It was more the euphoria that comes when you have faced a fierce challenge and coped. Storms are very different from other disasters at sea; they are much more emotional. With emergencies such as grounding, collision or fire, your responses are almost a mechanical process, apart of course from the shock. With a storm you see nature in the raw, and the experience is longer and much more drawn out. There is the build-up, the storm itself and the relief afterwards if all has gone well. Here the challenge is both mental and physical and your boat plays a big part in the process. This is life on the knife-edge, and if you haven't been out there you cannot fully appreciate the huge emotions that come from the drawn-out tension and excitement experienced in a storm.

Of course, when you are on that knife-edge you can cut yourself, but even then survival is still possible even with the odds stacked against you. Some of the tales of storm survival are quite remarkable, even though the odds against the crew were very high. These odds are much improved today and communications make it a less lonely experience, but storms still bring risks to vessels both large and small, and survival will initially depend on having a well-found ship underneath you.

There have been some excellent books written about small craft and storms, such as Adlard Coles' *Heavy Weather Sailing* and Steve Dashew's *Surviving the Storm*. Not only do these books recount the experiences of those challenged by severe storms at sea, but they serve as a guide to others who venture out on ocean passages. The majority of these storm experiences occur far from land, and any escape route to potential shelter has been blocked by distance or by the storm itself. Closer to land there may be the possibility of escape but weathering a storm in inshore waters can be a lot worse. Near land the effects of tides and shallow water add to the normal conditions of stormy seas, and there is also the worry of being close to a lee shore. Even modern yachts with their excellent sailing ability will have difficulty getting off a lee shore in storm conditions, even with an engine to help.

Big ships cracking up

Even big ships can suffer from storm damage. The container ship *Napoli* suffered severe cracks to her hull during a storm in the English Channel. The crew were taken off and the ship was beached. Worryingly, the winds were only blowing at about force 10 and the incident occurred in the English Channel, where the sea would not have built up to full storm proportions. If structural failure can happen to a big and supposedly well-designed ship in those conditions, what hope is there for small craft? In some ways the stresses on a big ship can be much greater than on a yacht. A large ship doesn't give; it has a more solid resistance to the waves. Then there is the speed factor – many modern container ships are capable of speeds of up to 25 knots, and they are expected to keep to fairly tight schedules. Trying to maintain higher speeds in rough seas can dramatically increase the stresses on the hull. Another container ship, the MSC *Carla,* was thought to have been travelling at too high a speed in rough sea in the Atlantic when she broke in two. Later examination of the hull concluded that there were weak welding points. The bulk carrier *Derbyshire* sank in a typhoon in the Pacific with the loss of all hands, and was also thought to have had a weakness in the hull that caused her to break in two.

Container ships also seem to be particularly vulnerable in storm conditions because of the high stack of cargo on deck. You can almost see the waves licking their lips when they see scontainers piled so high. If one of the container lashings goes, this then puts extra strain on the rest and the whole thing can come tumbling down like a pack of cards. A violent storm wrecked much of the deck cargo on the APL *Cina* when she was

on passage across the Pacific to the USA. As the vessel rolled and pitched heavily, containers were wrecked along the length of the ship, creating a major headache for the salvage teams who had to recover the debris. The *Ital Florida* was hit by waves up to 10m high when passing through the Arabian Sea at 16 knots and many of her container stacks collapsed. Late in 2007 the NYK *Antares* lost 52 containers overboard in a North Sea storm. While I do not believe that containers like this will float for long, in the short term they create a considerable hazard to small ships and boats.

This large container ship has had its container stack severely damaged in storm conditions. The loss of containers can create a threat to other vessels as well as making it very difficult to discharge the ones that are left on board.

Ferry disasters

Having to keep to schedules can be a recipe for disaster, and it is always a dilemma for ships' captains when balancing safety against the importance of the timetable. The ferry *Princess Victoria* was one of the first of the roll-on, roll-off ferries to operate in British waters, and at the end of January 1953 she sailed from Stranraer into the eye of a major storm. This was the same storm that decimated the east coast of England and Holland with severe flooding, and it could be argued that the *Princess Victoria* had no business sailing in those conditions. However, the tradition of maintaining the ferry service ruled. In the Force 12 winds, the vessel began to flood through the stern doors of the cargo deck. Water eventually entered the engine room and the vessel listed heavily. After about four hours she sank, taking 133 passengers and crew with her. It was Britain's worst ferry disaster until the *Herald of Free Enterprise* and is thought to have been caused by the failure of the stern doors.

These days ferries do cancel their operations when a severe storm is forecast, but this is usually because the very high-sided ships have difficulty in berthing safely when there is a very strong wind. During my lifeboat-testing days, I was taking a new American designed 44ft lifeboat to Holland to let the Dutch lifeboat crews have a look. We had run up the Channel overnight and went into Dover to refuel and get some breakfast. It was blowing about force 8 when we entered the harbour, but when it was time to leave, the wind had moved up a couple of notches to force 10 and the ferries had stopped their operations. Of course, our craft was a new design of lifeboat that needed storm experience, so off we sailed. Strong tides combined with a south-westerly storm and it was wild out there, with the seas very steep and unpredictable. We relied mainly on the radar for navigation in the poor visibility, but the picture disappeared when a huge wave wiped out the radar scanner from its mounting above the wheelhouse. I had already decided that we would head for Dunkerque rather than continue to Holland as the conditions were so severe, and eventually we came across a buoy that I thought would give us a fix. However, the entire top of the buoy had been swept away by the raging seas so there was no way to tell which buoy it was. The waves were not that big, probably around 15 to 20ft high, but they were steep and vicious. Finally we sighted land and crawled into Dunkerque, very battered and bruised. However, on that trip we had averaged 6 knots, which proved the lifeboat's capabilities. I was just thankful we were in a strong boat where nothing failed except that radar. I was also thankful that there were no ferries out in those conditions.

Ferry disasters increase

The number of ferry disasters around the world has reached worrying proportions. The majority of them have shifted to what we might consider the more remote parts of the world. Take Indonesia for instance. There have been seven reported ferry sinkings in the past three years, and that's just those caused by storms. Indonesia has perhaps the highest density of ferry routes in the world, for travel among the 17,000 islands that make up the archipelago. There are frequent storms in these waters, and one of the worst was in 2006; more than 400 were killed when a ferry broke up during a violent storm. In 2005 about 200 people were drowned when a ferry capsized in a storm in the seas off Eastern Indonesia. Most of the reports about these ferry disasters suggest that the ferries were overloaded and this is confirmed by the uncertain numbers of people who drowned because there are no definite passenger numbers.

Africa has also had its share of major ferry disasters. The *Bukoba* sank on Lake Victoria in a storm and over 1,000 died. The exact number of casualties was never known, but the ship was reported to be carrying twice its registered number of passengers, so overloading may have been a contributory cause. It was a similar story in 2002 when the *Joola* sank in a storm in the waters off Gambia. This was a fairly modern ship designed to carry 550 passengers but it is thought that there were over 2,000 on board at the time of the sinking. This ranks as one of the worst marine disasters of all time and local fishermen were only able to rescue 64 of the passengers. There seems little doubt that overloading was a contributory cause in both these accidents. Overloading weakens the defences of a ship by reducing stability when it encounters a storm, so it doesn't take much to cause the ship to succumb to the waves. It would seem to be a simple matter to control passenger numbers by simply placing a control on the gangway. Certainly on modern ferries operating in the developed world a passenger list is an essential part of the departure procedure, but obviously shipping control has a long way to go in many countries. Add to this the illegal shipping of migrants and it is hard to see any reduction in casualties occurring in the near future.

Back in 1954 there was a major ferry disaster in Japan when the *Toya Maru* was caught out in a typhoon. A typhoon is a pretty serious storm where winds can run up to 150mph or more. This typhoon was forecast, but the captain of the *Toya Maru* thought that it had passed through his area before he sailed. There were around 1,300 people on board. Shortly after departure, the conditions changed and the liner was anchored to let the typhoon pass. Unfortunately conditions deteriorated further, water entered the engine room via the car decks and the ship lost power, the anchor dragged and the captain decided to beach the liner in an attempt to save the passengers and crew. The high waves at the beaching point caused the ship to capsize and sink and only 150 survived.

Motorboats

Motorboats do not get caught out in storms with anything like the frequency of sailboats. This is because very few motorboats go out on ocean voyages as they don't have the fuel range. Coastal passages are the norm and weather forecasts will give early warning of any approaching storm, allowing the boat time to seek shelter. It might mean an uncomfortable passage as the seas rise, but a safe haven should be possible. This is just as well, because few motorboats these days are designed to survive extreme conditions. I would not like to be caught out in many of the motor yachts that I test for magazine reports. They are fine for the job they are designed to do, but that job is not to cope with wild and rough seas. There are exceptions

Conditions like this can be a challenge for both ships and small craft.

and we are starting to see a new breed of long range cruisers as owners become more adventurous. The VSV is a long thin hull, designed to be wave-piercing. Intended to go through waves rather than ride over them, I suspect this vessel could cope with extreme conditions. Although there is still the possibility of engine failure or human error, and power-boats do rely on their engines holding up to ensure survival. I have crossed the Atlantic a few times in motorboats trying to break records, but those crossings were done under what I would describe as 'controlled weather conditions'. You can be pretty sure of a weather forecast over the three- or four-day period needed, but we nearly got caught out on one attempt when a secondary low started to form. It was only our very high speed of 60 knots that allowed us to outrun it.

Boats like the VSV are built strongly to cope with the high stress of rough seas, but I think that some of the so-called long range cruising motor yachts could be at risk in very rough seas. Large areas of window; small scuppers to drain water away; electrical and mechanical systems that are not up to the highest standards can all make boats vulnerable. The same ought to be said about many of the sailboats out there. It is hard to picture them surviving the strength and power of a wall of breaking water that can envelop a boat in a storm. Any failures that allow water inside the boat will speed up the process of disaster. A boat can be built very sturdily and it will have a better chance of weathering a storm, but performance will tail off dramatically and for most sailors that would be an unacceptable compromise.

Problems of design

The advent of the Ro-Ro ferry has heralded quite a few disasters. The *Toya Maru* and the *Princess Victoria* were the forerunners of modern disasters and the warning signs were there for all to see. I can never understand how naval architects are allowed to put a door in the bow of a ship, just in the place where the structure should be at its sturdiest. It was failure of the bow doors on the *Estonia* that lead to it sinking in a storm in the Baltic with the loss of 852 lives. A fault was found in the design of the bow door which meant that under the stress of storm conditions, the outer door came loose. Though undoubtedly a serious problem, the ship should have retained her watertight integrity because there was an inner bow door that should also have been watertight. However, when the outer door was wrenched off, it damaged the inner door, scuppering that too. This meant that the ship was wide open to the sea at the bow, a sure recipe for disaster. From there on it was all downhill and the ship sank, but part of the blame was placed on the crew for their failure to appreciate the seriousness of the situation and the impact of the damage to the bow door.

This was a typical storm disaster scenario. The initial failure, while serious, should not have led to the ship sinking. It was compounded by a second resulting failure and a crew who did not want to believe that a big modern ship could fail in that way. The final straw was the severe cold of the Baltic winter and the great difficulty in launching any liferafts or lifeboats because of the dark and the extreme list. I am sure that there would have been panic of the highest order in such a terifying situation, and had I been on board, I would probably have been leading it. There is nothing quite like a ship nearly on her beam ends, in the dark, in a storm, to frighten people. Their world is literally turning upside down.

It is frightening to think that modern ships can still suffer in this way but it is important to realise that the design of ships is always going to be a compromise. It is not possible to build a ship that can cope with everything the sea might throw at it. The weak point on the *Estonia* was the bow doors; but it seems there is always something. Throughout history there are stories of ships being damaged in storms. Back in 1910 the liner *Lusitania* had her bridge windows smashed in by a freak wave in an Atlantic storm. As in the case of the *Estonia*, there are reports that the *Lusitania* was going too fast in order to meet a schedule. While her speed was suitable for average conditions, the ship was going too fast to cope when she encountered a higher than average wave. The Italian liner *Michelangelo* suffered a similar fate on the North Atlantic run in the 1950s, and the impact was big enough to damage part of the superstructure, resulting in the deaths of three passengers.

This is likely to be an increasing problem, as passenger ships are being designed to maximise passenger space and this has resulted in the high superstructures being carried further and further forward, presenting a bluff vertical face to any wave impact. The Cunard flagship *Queen Mary 2* has this layout but the designers say they have built in a huge strong breakwater over the foredeck so that any waves coming over the fine bow will be directed back overboard. It sounds like a much too simplistic solution to me; with such a fine bow shape and a speed of 30 knots this ship is going to be vulnerable to the 60ft plus freak waves that lurk in the North Atlantic in the winter. I forecast that within the next three years we will see reports of damage to this ship in violent seas. It will take fine judgement on the part of the captain to get the speed right for the conditions, when there are always rogue waves lurking and the pressure of a schedule to keep.

The cruise liner *Pacific Star* was recently damaged in a storm after leaving Auckland with 1,200 passengers on board. According to the experienced captain, the storm had been forecast but not its severity, and he told of wind blowing at 75 knots and gusting to 90 knots. The resulting 10m waves damaged the bow of the ship and broke many windows as well as taking the satcom dome overboard. That dome would have been about 80ft above the sea, and that distance shows how a wave coming on board can be accelerated as it passes up a sloping superstructure front before hitting the satcom dome, which would be one of the highest points on the ship.

The New Zealand passenger ship *Wahine* got caught out in a storm of ferocious proportions when on passage from Lyttelton in the South Island to Wellington at the southern end of the North Island. The Cook Straight between the two islands is a notorious bad weather region and the *Wahine's* passage here coincided with the passing of one of the most severe storms ever recorded in New Zealand. In winds nearing 100 knots the *Wahine* lost its radar and the waves were pushing it towards the Barrett Reef. The captain decided to head out to sea again but could not make progress, and the anchors were dropped to try to hold the ship. The winds continued to increase and the ship went aground at 06:40 in the morning. By 11:00 a harbour tug reached the stricken ship and tried to attach a line but the line parted and the ship swung round, allowing only four lifeboats to be launched before the ship capsized. Fifty-two people lost their lives in that storm, and the fate of *Wahine* is one of the earliest examples of water on the car deck causing a ship to capsize.

Rogue waves

Freak or rogue waves are recognised phenomena in open seas and modern research using satellites has shown that they are much more frequent than previously thought. The statistics for higher than average waves are quite frightening, and figures produced by the National Institute of Oceanography suggest one wave in 23 will be twice the average height of waves passing a fixed point. That is possible to cope with, but one wave in 1,175 will be three times the average height and one wave in 300,000 will be four times the average height.

In years at sea I have only twice knowingly encountered rogue waves. One occasion was off the coast of Iceland during the Cod War. We were in a storm in the middle of winter, a true North Atlantic storm of considerable ferocity, and we were running before the seas. I was spending some time out on the aft deck of our big ocean-going tug taking photos when a wave reared up astern and seemed to grow and grow. The crest was starting to break when I ran for cover to escape the foaming mass of water that crashed onto the low aft deck. I'd estimate that wave as being over 40ft high. The other time was on a lifeboat when we were searching for a man washed off the rocks on the north coast of Cornwall. My plan was to search from seaward looking inshore and I was prepared to go in among the breaking waves if we saw something, but not to take that risk when we were just searching. It was blowing force 8 from the north west so there was a considerable sea running, but we were quite happy outside the surf line; then it suddenly went dark. I looked around to seaward and could see the sun shining weakly through this great wall of water that had reared up to seaward of us! There was nothing I could do except watch the lifeboat rise like an express elevator up the side of the wave, then it promptly started to break as we passed through the crest onto the seaward side. That wave was certainly much bigger than the average that we were experiencing, and I should have made allowances for it, but our focus was on the search. It is easy to forget the danger that lurks out there.

That such rogue waves do exist can be seen from the wave recorder trace taken on board the Daunt Light Vessel off the south coast of Ireland. This shows a 42ft wave crest among waves that are only averaging around 12ft.

Before you give up boating after reading these figures, let's examine them a little more closely. Firstly that average wave height is probably lower than you might think when looking at wave trains. You tend to judge a sea by the height of the larger waves, so those waves that are twice the average height would be included in your general assessment. Secondly, if you take a wave period of

This ship is about to encounter a rogue wave. The wave crest is probably three times the height of the average wave, but can be even larger.

A larger wave than normal crashes on board a ship at sea. The sheer force of the breaking water can cause damage that makes the ship more vulnerable in storm conditions.

10 seconds between the wave crests, which could be the average for a rough sea, then there are 6 waves per minute, 360 waves per hour and 14,400 waves per day. This means that the chances of meeting that one wave in 300,000 are fairly remote, particularly when you remember that such a rogue wave would be a transient wave, appearing and disappearing quite quickly. These enormous waves tend to be caused by the interaction of crossing or different wave trains and when this happens, the height of the two individual crests is combined to create the higher crest. The four times average height wave might be caused by the interaction of three wave trains at that one point in the ocean, so you could see it but not experience it as it will have disappeared before it reaches you.

It is daunting to think that 40ft waves can be encountered among those that are averaging just 10ft in height. Such waves are likely to be more of a danger to big ships than to small boats, because the big ship does not necessarily have the resilience to lift to the wave and will tend to force its way through it. The higher the speed, the greater the impact, and in those situations it is the sea that always wins. Slowing down in severe conditions is the obvious way to reduce vulnerability to storm wave damage, but how much do you need to slow down to be safe? You must also be careful that you do not slow down to the point where steerage control is lost. This aspect of design affects both ships and boats and would seem to be a fruitful area of research for each new design, so that the captains would at least have a guide they could work to.

Wave troughs

Another hazard to watch for in storm conditions is the deep trough that may accompany a rogue wave. That trace from the Daunt Light Vessel shows the trough before the high crest and if a boat falls into that trough before encountering the high peak there is every chance that the breaking crest of the high wave will fall on the boat. It might be possible to see a high crest arriving when it is still a few waves away but that deep trough will not be visible until you fall into it. I came across one of these deep troughs in the tide race off Portland Bill when testing a lifeboat in wild seas. As it turned out, I was going too fast for the conditions and we came over this crest to see a deep, deep hole on the other side. I'm sure you could almost see the seabed down there and the whole boat became airborne as it dropped into the trough with a resounding crash. If we hadn't been in a lifeboat I am sure that the hull would have been damaged by the impact. Certainly those on board were all shaken by the experience and lucky not to have been injured. That boat was wired with stress gauges to see just what a lifeboat has to withstand in rough seas, and one of my reasons for going into those seas was to find out. All the gauges went off the scale, which gives some idea of what a boat can experience in storm conditions.

Even big ships can be affected by these deep troughs, and they are thought to have been the cause of a number of accidents to large tankers making the passage around the Cape of Good Hope. This is an area that is thought to be particularly susceptible to rogue waves because here the south-west-going Agulhas Current meets the severe storms that sweep to the east around the Southern Ocean. Any wind against current situation will see more severe conditions, with steeper and higher waves. When that current reaches up to 3 knots with the wind blowing up to force 10 with an unlimited fetch, then you have the recipe for wild and dangerous seas. When the tankers encountered the rogue waves and deep troughs, and these accidents started to happen, my reaction was to wonder why the experts seemed to find it unexpected. These extreme sea conditions can be found in many areas of the world where there is a wind against current or tide; the Portland Race in the English Channel is a well known example. In the United States, the sea conditions deteriorate rapidly when a northerly wind meets the north-going Gulf Stream, off the east coast.

Extreme storms

The seas generated by hurricanes, typhoons and similar tropical storms have to be seen to be believed. As far as the seaman is concerned these are the ultimate storms, but they generally only occur in tropical or subtropical waters and only in certain seasons of the year. Anyone who has experienced one of these storms will not forget it in a hurry and my everlasting experience of a hurricane came off the coast of Central America. It was impossible to tell where the sea ended and the sky began. There was just a maelstrom of wind and water, and we felt that we were virtually enveloped in solid water, despite being above it. You almost feel you are drowning when you try to breathe.

I was on a cargo ship and we had just come down to a speed that would maintain steerage way when we entered the storm. Visibility was about zero so it was impossible to judge the size of the waves. Nevertheless, we knew they were big when one came on board and flattened the two lifeboats on the weather side of the ship, rendering them completely unusable. They would not have been much use anyway, because there is no way a ship's lifeboat would survive those conditions, even if it could be launched safely. We rode out that storm for 36 hours and the ship and crew came out battered but still intact. It is not difficult to imagine how one small failure of a critical system on board could begin a spiral towards disaster in those conditions.

The second hurricane I experienced was in port in Cuba, and I would much rather be at sea in a hurricane than in port. Certainly you receive more reports of boats being damaged in harbour than you do at sea, but then there are many more boats sheltering in harbour during a hurricane, so the statistics do not mean much.

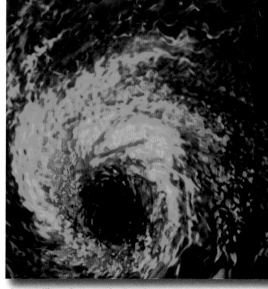

A satellite picture of a hurricane, showing the well–defined circular pattern of the clouds and the wind.

Extreme storms of this kind are not limited to tropical waters. Storms of similar ferocity can be found further north and south. While they may not have quite the level of extreme winds they tend to extend over a larger area and so can be just as dangerous. When in extreme conditions, it is impossible to tell the difference between a wind of 90 knots and one of 120 knots. At both wind strengths, the seas will be severe and seamen will be in survival mode.

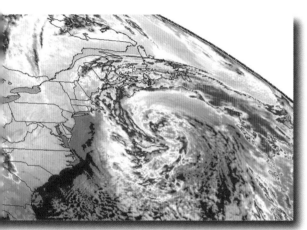

The phrase refers to the simultaneous occurrence of events that, taken individually, would be far less powerful than the result of their chance combination.

The Perfect Storm

The Perfect Storm off the coast of north-eastern America was an example of how such extreme conditions can develop. This will often be when two or more deepening low-pressure areas start to merge together. The result is the starting point of a depression that becomes deeper and deeper with resulting winds that can match a hurricane in ferocity. This type of storm can be notoriously difficult to forecast because it is relatively rare, and the computer modelling does not feature much historical data about them. Forecasters will probably only be aware of the scale of the developing depression after it has become severe, but that is not much consolation to any mariners out at sea, as the crew of the *Andrea Gail* found out. An equally intense storm, but much smaller in scale, developed in the English Channel after the forecasters notoriously said that reports of a severe storm developing were not true. The barograph trace on the destroyer HMS *Birmingham,* which was out in the storm helping with the rescue of a catamaran, went off the bottom of the scale to show one of the lowest barometer readings ever recorded.

A dip of such severity would be almost impossible to forecast and could be quite localised, but the winds generated would be extremely violent. To all intents these are would-be hurricane conditions. I loved the laconic comment of the captain of HMS *Birmingham* when he said that his anemometer would not register over 90 knots of wind, so he did not know what the wind strength actually was. The ship was rolling violently in the wild seas, and then in a matter of minutes the wind direction swung through 90 degrees. They were obviously very close to the centre of this intense depression and it was impressive that in these very severe conditions the Weymouth lifeboat was able to take off the crew of the catamaran that was in trouble. Because the intensity of this storm had not been fully appreciated there were several yachts out that October night in 1987, and severe damage in the South of England when the storm hit land.

100 knot winds

I have been in a North Atlantic storm where the wind reached 100 knots before the anemometer broke. This was on an 80ft long catamaran when we were trying to set a record under sail across the Atlantic. We wanted strong winds for the record, but this was much more than we had bargained for and we were down to bare poles and streaming warps to try to slow the boat down but we were still running before the wind at 10 knots. It was a frightening experience because we felt so out of control, and the stress of that storm created cracks in the hull which led to us eventually having to be rescued (as recounted in the Rescues chapter). Those stress cracks got steadily larger and the boat was literally bending in the middle. We knew that it would only be a short time before the hulls broke in two and the boat capsized, which was why we decided to call for help. The cracks were letting in water and, of course, that was when the bilge pumps decided to stop working. We had to resort to bailing out the hulls by bucket but between bailing there was time to get some rest, knowing that there were going to be some very stressful times ahead. We invented a new bilge alarm system during these rest periods. Because some of the crew were sleeping on inflatable mattresses in the bottom of the boat, when these began to float and bump into things we knew it was time to start bailing again.

When you are in a severe storm, it seems that the world has gone out of control. The wind rises and the seas become wild and extreme. And just when you think it cannot get any worse, that this is the strongest wind you have ever known, the wind speed rises another notch. Then you get the desperate feeling that you can't stand any more and that things can't get any worse, but they do and everything goes off the scale of experience. There is a sense of resignation because there is so little you can do at this stage except hope and pray. However, it is amazing how both boats and crews can go through such extreme storms and come out the other end, back into a world of relative normality.

Racing disasters

Some, however, do not survive and the record of ocean racing and severe storms is not good. The Fastnet Race storm of 1979 remains fixed in everyone's memory as the turning point in ocean racing, when the organisers had to face up to whether it was safe for yachts to race in open ocean conditions. The enquiry into the 15 deaths that occurred during this race showed that many modern yacht designs were just not suitable for coping with severe conditions. There was particular concern about the range of stability on a number of the yachts, with some running out of stability at an angle of 120 degrees. This meant they were prone to a full capsize with just a knock down. The actual strength of many yachts was also called into question and I have always felt that you are on the downhill path to disaster when something breaks on board. When one thing breaks it puts added stress on other parts of the boat, but more importantly it puts added stress on the crew who are trying to correct the problem or even just trying to cope. That is when more things are likely to go wrong, and when you read accounts from survivors you can see the deterioration taking place.

The lessons of the Fastnet Race disaster do not seem to have been learnt. In 1984 another severe storm that was not forecast caused havoc among the 30 entries in a race from Durban to East London in South Africa. Here the yachts were sailing with the powerful Agulhas Current helping them along, but the 60 knot winds of the storm were blowing against the current. These conditions generate very short, steep seas that yachts find hard to cope with. One yacht was lost without trace, three others were rolled through 360 degrees and one was blown ashore. The enquiry called into question the suitability of the modern racing yacht design to cope with extremes.

The weakness of many modern yacht designs was highlighted again in the 1991 race from Japan to Guam. On the yacht *Marine Marine* the downhill slope to disaster started when one crewman was lost overboard and not recovered. A second crewmember suffered extreme seasickness and was taken off by a

Storm force winds can result in severe damage to a yacht.

patrol boat. In the rough seas, *Marine Marine* decided to abandon racing but could not start the engine as a rope was wound round the propeller. Then they noticed that the yacht was developing an unusual rolling motion. In the dark the keel had dropped off and the yacht capsized, drowning seven members of the crew, and leaving just one survivor. Another yacht, the *Taka*, also capsized but all the crew, except one, managed to board the liferaft. Unfortunately their EPIRB did not work and despite extensive searches that liferaft was not found until the best part of a month later; only one of the survivors was still alive.

The weather conditions for this race disaster were not particularly severe, with winds of 30 knots gusting to 50; the sort of conditions that might be found in any average gale. The loss of yacht keels does seem to be becoming an increasing problem. This must be a cause for concern, particularly with some of the more extreme yacht designs that are now participating in very long distance and around the world ocean races. Yacht designers are being pushed to produce designs with ever-increasing performance and weight is a critical factor in high performance yachts. The designers must pare the weight down to a minimum to give the best performance, while at the same time designing a yacht that will cope with the worst conditions found in the wild Southern Ocean. It is hard to know just where the limits are from the perspective of a drawing board. Sailors know precisely where the limits are when they find them, but by then it is too late.

The famous Sydney to Hobart Race in Australia has been hit by bad weather several times. The 1998 race was one of the worst, when a low pressure area developed in the Bass Strait between the Australian mainland and Tasmania as the yachts were approaching the area. Again this low was not shown in any of the longer term forecasts, but it brought winds of 70 knots or more over a 10-hour period and decimated the racing fleet. Six people died and 55 had to be rescued, and once again several of the yachts sank through structural failures. Again, it does seem that lessons are not learnt and you can see the temptation to push the performance limits in a race that is held in the summer months when, in theory, the weather should be fine. It is interesting to note that both this race and the 1979 Fastnet were summer races and yet both produced storms that developed at very short notice. Storms are expected in the winter months, yet the very challenging ones appear to come in the summer, when everyone has a more relaxed attitude towards the weather.

Cruising yachts

Cruising yachts appear to have a more conservative approach to design than racing yachts, because they are not seeking the same level of performance. There are many tales of cruising yachts coping with extreme conditions and surviving but, as always, we only tend to hear about those who did survive and not those who were lost. It amazes me that people set out on a world cruise aboard what are basically production yachts, and that they survive and cope despite experiencing severe storms. However, I think that there is a considerable difference between severe and very severe storms, and this is where the prospects of survival lie. Most well-found and well-prepared sailing yachts could cope with a severe storm, but would encounter difficulties in very severe conditions. When you move onto the very severe level, you enter the unknown. The level of stress and strain on the yacht, its gear and, most importantly, its crew become extreme. That is when you become vulnerable and the sea starts to find your weak points.

More severe storms to come

Storms at sea are an incredible experience and they can be very challenging even for the best-designed modern ships and boats. There are forecasts that storms will become more severe and more frequent with the changes brought about by global warming and already some of the oil platforms in the North Sea that were built to withstand the '100-year wave' are finding that they are experiencing such waves at more frequent intervals. That '100-year wave' should be the most extreme event that only occurs every 100 years or not at all, but these theoretical monster waves are now arriving perhaps every ten years. There are huge waves out there and it only requires the right combination of natural events and being in the wrong place at the wrong time to come across them.

If you haven't experienced a storm at sea then your boating experience is not complete. It is natural and safest to run away from storms and seek shelter if that option is open to you; nobody goes out looking for storms, except when testing lifeboats, but they are part and parcel of normal sea-going. Even with the best technology and forecasting expertise, predicting storms is far from an exact science, as some of the experiences mentioned in this chapter have shown, so you can never be sure that you will not have to cope with one. They affect ships and boats, large and small, and even when they are forecast there is no way that these storms can be controlled. Storms at sea are nature at its wildest and we are still in the infancy of learning how to cope with them and of developing the technology that will guarantee survival.

MARINE ACCIDENT INVESTIGATION BRANCH

Knockdown and total loss off the Portuguese Coast

Narrative

An 11.3m sailing yacht was being used for an intensive 13 week Yachtmaster training course. The instructor and four crew had already spent almost two months on board sailing on the south coast of England and then to the Channel Islands, Brittany and western France before heading across the Bay of Biscay for Spain and Portugal in mid-November. By this time, the students had amassed a good deal of experience and the instructor decided it was time for them to skipper the yacht without him being on board. A passage of around 75 miles southwards down the coast was planned, and the instructor stepped ashore. Winds were forecast to be a force 4 westerly, veering northerly force 5.

However, while on passage, the winds increased to gale force from the north-west. The skipper on board phoned the instructor ashore and it was agreed that the original destination was going to be too dangerous to approach in the prevailing conditions as there was a bar at the harbour entrance and the pilot book suggested this may be unsafe. An alternative destination was agreed, which was thought to offer a safer approach but which was another 30 miles further south.

The designated skipper became incapacitated with seasickness as the severe conditions continued, so another student (the most experienced of the four) took over. With sails furled and the engine on, they made their approach but were knocked down to an estimated 110 degrees by a breaking wave.

The acting skipper was on the helm and was washed overboard. He had been clipped on but was unable to get back on board. The next wave took the yacht past the harbour entrance, and shortly afterwards she hit the beach. The acting skipper suffered cracked ribs, but he and the rest of the crew were otherwise unscathed. The yacht was damaged beyond repair.

The Lessons

1

The decision to continue to an alternative port further south was understandable, but an approach to any port on a lee shore in the prevailing conditions carried risks. Although unpalatable to the crew, staying out at sea would probably have saved the yacht. The MAIB has looked into other accidents where the crew were less fortunate, and such action would have saved lives.

2

Leaving experienced students aboard without their instructor has the value of ensuring that the skipper knows he or she really is in charge, and must stand or fall by the decisions made. However, the instructor should carry out a particularly thorough risk assessment with the full involvement of the students.

Survival

There are many remarkable tales of survival at sea which demonstrate just how resilient and determined seafarers can be when faced with disaster. What will never be known is just how many people suffered a shipwreck in storms or collisions and did not survive. Some tales of survival show seafarers enduring long periods in small open boats, but was there an equal number who took to their liferafts, and despite surviving for days or even months were not picked up? Such events go unrecorded in the annals of disaster because no record can be kept, and this is a haunting thought for all those who venture out to sea.

Ships' lifeboats saved many lives in the Second World War and some epic journeys were made in open lifeboats like this.

Wartime

Wartime and the considerable number of ships sunk by enemy action was probably one of the main instigators of ships' crews taking to lifeboats and entering survival mode. Once again there are some remarkable tales of long voyages made under extreme conditions to finally make landfall, but how many of these seamen did not live to tell the tale? The sudden and explosive nature of the sinking of these ships means the abandon ship process would have been carried out in a hurry with little time for collecting the correct clothing, equipment and provisions. Inevitably some crew members would be injured and thus have a greatly reduced chance of survival. Injury is the sort of stress you can do without when trying to survive, but these men had no choice. For every survival story we hear of man's more basic instincts taking over, there is another filled with caring, compassionate events.

I was lucky to start my sea-going career shortly after the Second World War had ended. When I was a young apprentice, we had a chief officer who had lived through the war. When his ship was torpedoed, he spent 47 days in a lifeboat with members of the crew. In this epic of survival, our chief officer finally got the lifeboat across the Indian Ocean to land, living off rainwater and what the sea could offer. One of the most remarkable aspects of this long voyage was that the chief officer constructed a sextant from one of the empty lifeboat biscuit tins, enabling him to navigate in a very rudimentary way. Without a timepiece, the navigation was based mainly on establishing the latitude from noon sights, but that, combined with dead reckoning and using the basic charts supplied on wartime lifeboats, enabled them to reach land. One of the biggest problems faced in a lifeboat or liferaft is having nothing to occupy one's mind. I was incredibly grateful to have my cameras with me when in the liferaft after the sinking of the *Virgin Atlantic Challenger*. Making that sextant and having to work on the navigation must have been very therapeutic.

Lifeboat survival

It was a similar story when the tanker *Athel Knight* was sunk in the Atlantic. Only two lifeboats got away from the ship with 33 crewmembers on board. The second officer was in charge of one and he decided to head for the nearest land, which was Antigua in the West Indies, 1,100 miles away. Navigating with just the lifeboat's compass, an alarm clock and a pencil, it took 38 days to reach land. This landfall was made just 60 miles away from the planned point. The same second officer, Mr Crook, was rescued a second time, but on this occasion was able to reboard the ship and get the engines started again.

Eight years before the *Titanic* hit an iceberg and sank, the Norwegian immigrant ship *Norge* hit a reef in the Atlantic off the isolated rock of Rockall. Like the *Titanic,* there were insufficient lifeboats for the 800 people on board and over 600 of them lost their lives. One lifeboat, designed for 48, had 72 people crammed on board and it was five days before they were picked up by a trawler and landed ashore. One of the lifeboats made a remarkable voyage; the officer in charge miscalculated his navigation and, instead of heading for the nearby Scottish coast, made landfall in the Faroe Islands many miles to the north. Fortunately it was summer when the shipwreck occurred so exposure was less of a problem, but that lifeboat journey must remain one of the more stressful and lucky voyages in history.

In this modern age, where good communications and emergency beacons should inform the authorities of boats in trouble, there should not be any epic lifeboat journeys like this. Any ship in trouble ought to be able to send a message of distress. With yachts the story may be different and any disaster can be much more immediate and devastating. There have been a number of incredible survival stories told by the crews of yachts that have suddenly met with disaster. The record for survival at sea is held by the Bailey family who survived for 117 days in a small dinghy. This does not sound that long, but translate it into nearly four months or one third of a year and it sounds like an eternity. Theirs is a remarkable survival story and it shows what can be endured when things go wrong.

Some of the survivors from the Norge *endured an epic journey after the ship caught fire and the officer in charge of the lifeboat got his navigation wrong.*

Sunk by a whale

It was in 1973, and the Baileys were on a cruise from England to New Zealand in their 31ft wooden yacht when they encountered a whale that put a hole in the hold of the boat. With little time to spare, they abandoned ship into a liferaft and a rubber dinghy, taking minimal supplies: a sextant, a compass, some repair kit for the boats, and some water containers. They survived on rainwater and

There is no guarantee that you will be seen when you set off a flare.

by catching fish, seabirds and turtles. They passed the time by playing dominoes and cards, designing their replacement yacht, and planning what they would eat when they got ashore. It was this positive thinking that kept them going, but their health was gradually deteriorating, with painful sores appearing on their bodies. The dinghy capsized three times in storms, they lost some of their equipment and towards the end they could barely move. They had waved madly at passing ships but were not seen. Finally a Korean fishing boat sighted them and picked them up after 117 days adrift.

Adrift

Many survivors speak of the huge anticipation when a ship is sighted and then the awful drop in morale when it sails past without seeing the tiny boats in the huge ocean. It must be almost impossible to recover from that disappointment, to feel that this is the end, that no one cares, but as a survivor you have little choice. There is simply not the luxury of options; survivors must take what is on offer and make the most of it. Having flares to attract attention can provide a psychological boost, but the temptation is to use them all at once when a ship is first sighted, and there is no guarantee the flares will be seen. Keeping a visual lookout tends to be way down on the list of priorities for any officer on watch aboard a ship. The chances of being spotted by a modern ship are minimal. In over a third of ship-to-ship collisions, one ship did not see the other until just before impact. What chance is there that they will see a liferaft?

The Baileys had each other for support and it should have been the same for Bill and Simmone Butler, who had a similar experience with whales. Their yacht *Siboney* was holed and sank, and they spent 66 days in a liferaft before being rescued. Accounts suggest that the couple were not on the best of terms before disaster struck. They were then ravaged by thirst, racked with hunger and battered by storms before their eventual rescue by a passing patrol boat of the Costa Rican Coastguard. By that time they had drifted closer to land, but 66 days in a liferaft trying to persuade yourself you will be rescued is not easy when the biggest struggle is merely to stay alive.

Another amazing survival story comes from Tami Ashcroft who, along with her boyfriend, was delivering a yacht from Tahiti to San Diego. They encountered a hurricane and in huge seas the yacht was capsized and pitch-poled. Ashcroft was down below and only regained consciousness after 27 hours. She woke to find the safety line securing her boyfriend in the cockpit trailing astern. Weak from blood loss and mourning for her boyfriend, she did nothing for two days, then set up a jury rig. She was able to fix her position with a sextant and it took 42 days to sail the boat single-handed to Hawaii. That is a considerable achievement and must have required focus and determination.

None of us can know how we would behave in such circumstances, and of course, we have only the accounts of those who did survive to reference. How many others were shipwrecked in similar circumstances and did not survive?

No EPIRB?

Modern communications do not always provide the answer. Very recently a couple spent eight days drifting in a liferaft after their yacht *Gigo 2* capsized and sank in stormy seas in the Indian Ocean. The couple, an Italian man and an Israeli woman, were sailing from the Maldives to the Red Sea when their yacht sank. They took to the liferaft with just emergency rations. They were spotted by a Belgian tug 650 miles off the coast of Kochi and were suffering from severe dehydration, sickness and skin problems, demonstrating just how quickly a survivor's health can deteriorate on a liferaft in tropical conditions. However, their real problem was that they had no EPIRB or other means of indicating their distress situation. Without that, rescue is a matter of luck rather than planning.

Being on your own in a liferaft must be even worse because you have no one there to give any moral support. Steve Callahan spent 76 days adrift in a liferaft after his yacht sank six days out from the Canary Islands. The trade winds in that area continued to carry him across the Atlantic rather than returning him to the land he had just left and he travelled around 1,800 miles in that liferaft, which must be some sort of record. Callahan was lucky in that he had a solar still in the liferaft which provided continuous supplies of fresh water. Like others, he caught fish but when rescued he had lost a tremendous amount of weight and was badly sunburned. He put his survival down to his experience as a sailor and a boatbuilder and to a very positive attitude.

In the water

So far we have looked at survivors who have been lucky enough to take to their liferaft or dinghy. How much worse must it be to find yourself in the water with virtually no means of support? From a position in the water the ocean looks vast, and the temptation to slip beneath the surface and end the challenge must be huge. However, people do endure and Lillian Simpson spent 19 hours surviving before being rescued off Hawaii. She was tipped into the water when her kayak capsized and had only a small flotation device to cling to. Simpson says that she slept during the long night as she floated in the sea and was even asleep when the fishing boat that rescued her came alongside. Trying to spot someone floating in the water is one of the biggest challenges for rescuers, but the crew of this fishing boat were not even searching for her, so they must have been keeping a very good lookout.

When I was working with the lifeboats, I came across another remarkable survival story. I arrived on the island of Jersey in the aftermath of a huge storm. This had resulted in a motor yacht being overwhelmed by big seas on the approach to St Helier, the main port. There are very strong tidal currents around the island that make the seas even more dangerous, and the boat's whole superstructure had been ripped off when it was hit by a big breaking wave. The three crew ended up in the water clinging to bits of wreckage; a girl in her 20s and her parents. Her parents could not endure the cold and the encroaching darkness and they slipped away and drowned, but the girl kept going and drifted with the wind and tide. At one point during the night she thought the shore lights looked close enough to swim for shore. She let go of the piece of wood that was keeping her afloat and headed for the lights. It was much further than she thought, and now she was alone and trying to keep afloat. Eventually, after 18 hours adrift, she finally made it to shore where she was faced with a 200ft climb up the cliffs. The lifeboat had been out all night searching for survivors when the empty remains of the yacht had been discovered, but the sole survivor was only found when she knocked on the door of a farmhouse. I saw her in hospital the next day when she was partly recovered. At that time she could not explain what had motivated her to survive that long night in dark and wild seas. She had travelled halfway around the island, much of it without any support except her amazing will to survive.

Sharks

Being adrift in the water takes on a terrifying new dimension when there are sharks around. Experienced sailor Debbie Kiley and four other crew were on a delivery trip from Maine to Florida in a 58ft sailboat when they got caught in a storm. After a stopover in Maryland they continued south and encountered an even more severe storm. Winds of up to 60 knots were reported and waves stood up to 45ft tall. The yacht became flooded and started to sink, so they inflated the liferaft, but it blew away. Next they tried to get into the inflatable tender but it kept turning over in the strong wind, so the crew were left in the water holding on to the tender. After 18 hours in the water the wind eased, and they righted the tender and climbed in. Only then did they become aware of the sharks that were surrounding the boat.

By the third day the crew were starting to fall apart and some began to drink seawater. Two of the crew went overboard to try to warm up in the balmy Gulf Stream water and were eaten by the sharks. One female crewmember died in the night from the wounds she had suffered during the storm, leaving just two remaining crew, who were now nearing the end. Finally they were rescued by a passing Russian ship, but even that was traumatic. Here is a tale of survival that went horribly wrong. The reports suggest that the crew simply weren't mentally equipped to cope. The mental instability that can come from being thrust into a survival situation is infectious. The situation will only be made worse by the inevitable onset of seasickness that comes after taking to a small boat or a liferaft. I know from my experience in the liferaft after *Virgin Atlantic Challenger* sank that some of the crew were seasick after just half an hour.

In what was an amazing rescue, four men fishing for sharks found themselves in the water when their boat was swamped by a big wave. The boat went down so fast that none of them had the chance to grab lifejackets and there they were in the water, without support and with sharks circling round. One of the men found a cooler box that had floated out of the boat and inside this was a mobile phone that had been wrapped in a plastic bag. They were able to send out an emergency call to the Coastguard before the phone went dead and were rescued within 90 minutes. With sharks in the water that must have been the longest 90 minutes of their lives.

Preparation

We hear of so many cases like this where the crews of yachts and motorboats have been overtaken by disaster and find they are insufficiently prepared to cope. It is a huge shock to encounter disaster at sea and this makes it hard to cope with the enormity of events. Professionals, however, approach high-risk ventures with a very different mindset. These seamen know that safety margins have been reduced and are prepared both mentally and with superior survival equipment.

Take the case of Phil Weld, an experienced long-distance sailor who became famous for his

Phil Weld was a very experienced long-distance sailor and had a very professional approach to survival.

winning ways in his trimarans *Moxie* and *Gulf Streamer*. He was sailing *Gulf Streamer* across the Atlantic to participate in the single-handed transatlantic race when he was hit by a storm and the boat capsized. He and fellow crewman Bill Stephens spent five days in the upturned trimaran before being rescued. There is no hint of panic or desperation in their account of the survival, just a case of making the best out of what was available. They tried to ensure that their upturned boat would be sighted in the best way and generally coped well with a situation that was beyond their control. It was five days before rescue came, but they were preparing for a much longer stay in the upturned boat just in case. This capsize happened in the early days of EPIRBs, when they operated only on aircraft frequencies, so sending out distress messages from the upturned boat was not an option.

Tony Bullimore had the same approach when the keel sheared off his monohull racing yacht in the Southern Ocean. Without its keel the boat capsized, but there was enough air inside the hull for Bullimore to survive. He ensured that his EPIRB was operating correctly and simply waited patiently for rescue, which came after three days. The Southern Ocean is a lonely place and it was an Australian navy ship that found Bullimore after homing in on the EPIRB signal.

The 1979 Fastnet race

A truly epic tale of survival is that of one of the crew in the fateful Fastnet race of 1979, when a violent and unforecast storm played havoc with the large fleet of racing yachts. Out of the 303 yachts that started the race, only 85 reached the finish line, 5 sank and 19 were abandoned. The storm hit the fleet of yachts just when they were most vulnerable, in the open waters of the Western Approaches, on their way to the Fastnet Rock off the south-west corner of Ireland. Nick Ward was one of the crew on board *Grimalkin*. Three of the crew managed to take to the liferaft after a discussion about whether to stay with the dismasted yacht or use the tender. One of the crew was swept away and Nick himself was washed overboard, but was held by his safety harness and hauled himself back on board. When he recovered consciousness he found only one crew member left and hauled him aboard. That man later died, and Nick was left alone with the body to face a traumatic ordeal before being rescued. The three who took to the liferaft survived. This is just one tale out of many on that traumatic day that will live on in the memory of anyone involved with ocean racing.

Exaggerated survival?

One 'survival' event that I was involved in turned out not to be a survival story at all, but an attempt to defraud an insurance company. The story began when a Greek gentleman decided to take his large sports cruiser to one of the Greek islands, where he intended to visit a special chapel to pray for his wife who was ill. He set off from Piraeus together with his crewman on the planned two-hour trip to the island. It was getting dark as they left and the wind was blowing force 7 but among the islands there was not a huge sea running and they said they were steaming at around 25 knots.

According to the report filed with the insurance company, when they were halfway to their destination the owner saw that a large fender had been left out over the stern. He attempted to haul it on board and in doing so lost his footing and fell overboard but managed to grab the fender rope. The crewman was talking on the radio at the time and saw the owner go over; he quickly reported the problem over the radio then rushed aft to help. Unfortunately, he too went overboard and at that moment the fender rope broke. Both men were now in the water and the boat was disappearing over the horizon under autopilot control. The crewman swam back, following the line of the disappearing stern light of the boat, and met up with the owner who was by that time clinging to the large fender. The story goes that they spent the whole night clinging to the fender, and when dawn came they were rescued by one of the owner's ferries that had been diverted to search. The search was instigated by the boat that the crewman had been talking to on the VHF radio. It was a remarkable survival story: the men clung to that fender all night in very rough conditions and the boat was never seen again. The problem was that the insurance company did not believe the story when a claim was put in for the loss of the boat.

There were many aspects of this story that did not seem plausible, but there was nothing in the account that definitely could not have happened. The insurance company simply felt there were too many coincidences for it to be true, added to the fact that there was no trace of the boat, even though it was heading towards land when last seen. I came in to act as an expert when the owner took the insurance company to court to claim his money. Our lawyer thought we had a strong case even though there was no conclusive proof that the events did not happen as stated. It was after three weeks in court that the owner let something slip in the witness box. After the fender rope parted, he claimed to have swum to the fender some 25m away. In a force 7 wind that fender would have been going downwind so fast that even if he had been an Olympic swimmer the owner could not have caught up with it. As survival stories go it was amazing, but sadly it was not true and the claim was not paid.

Piracy

Another intriguing survival story is that of the two men found in a liferaft by the US Coastguard, in the waters between Florida and the Bahamas. This discovery followed the finding of a Miami charter boat, *Joe Cool,* drifting at sea with no one on board. The ensuing search found two men in the liferaft together with their luggage, US$2,000 in cash, knives and blow dart apparatus. There was no sign of the other four crewmembers who had been on board and the two survivors are now being charged with piracy on the high seas, under suspicion that they murdered the crew. The story becomes more complicated because the drifting boat was found way off course, near the coast of Cuba, which would have meant that it had drifted against the prevailing Gulf Stream. Piracy has been a major problem in the waters off the south of the United States, much of it associated with drugs in one way or another. The *Joe Cool* case continues to unfold.

Does water make a soft landing?

Survival stories like this keep the action on the water. At least when a yacht is abandoned for a liferaft it is the same environment, no matter how difficult the circumstances may be. Imagine what it must be like when an aircraft has to ditch and the crew are in the water, trying to survive in a totally different environment. Today it is rare to hear of modern airliners ditching and when the cabin crew go through the motions of demonstrating the lifejacket, 'In the unlikely event of landing on water', don't be fooled. There is virtually no chance of survival. The landing speed of a modern airliner is just too high and the water impact would be so severe that the plane would break up and sink rapidly.

Light aircraft are a different matter and there are several recent accounts of these planes ditching and the crew surviving. In 1997 the four-man crew of a single-engined aircraft were on a flight to Mexico when engine failure and bad weather forced them to ditch. They sent out a Mayday but received no response and then they were in the water.

When a light aircraft ditches in the water the crew first have to survive ditching and then the wait for rescue.

Fortunately they had lifejackets and a cooler box that offered some buoyancy. The seas were estimated at 8 to 10ft and the water was relatively warm. After a couple of hours they saw a helicopter, but it turned away. Land was in sight in the distance and one crewmember decided to swim there to get help. He made it to shore at around 02:30 and found some fishermen, but they had no means of communication. Despite this, they took the survivor out by boat the next morning and put a search into operation. After nearly 24 hours in the water, the rest of the crew were picked up by a Mexican navy patrol boat.

A matter of luck

These examples of survival show that in virtually all rescues there is a huge amount of luck involved. Every situation is different and much will depend on what equipment is available once the ship or aircraft has been abandoned. The speed at which evacuation takes place will also have a bearing on survival. The difficulty lies in making decisions about what to take, when to leave and what to do without having any knowledge about what lies ahead. The transition from pleasant sailing to survival can be sudden, and it is likely the sailor will have very little experience in coping with the situation. When I read the many survival stories it seems to me that a survival suit must be considered a priority. Even the men who ditched near Mexico were becoming hypothermic when they were rescued and that was in relatively warm water. In colder waters a survival suit is essential, but many are poorly designed and take time to put on – time that is not always available in an emergency. The suits can also restrict the movement and agility that may be important in an abandon ship situation.

Liferafts

Liferafts can be a poor substitute for a comfortable yacht or ship but they do provide a measure of protection and survival in an emergency. They will also almost certainly make you seasick and, from my limited experience, I would always recommend a seasickness pill. Seasickness is most debilitating, and destroys the will to survive, so the pill and the survival suit are the two essentials in my book. These are closely followed by some means of communication, an EPIRB and/or a waterproof radio. This list could go on and on, but it is essential to give the matter some thought even though you may not be planning a hazardous journey. The more I read other people's survival stories, the more I realise that the vast majority were unprepared for their ordeal, and that inevitably made things worse.

Preparation with training and safety courses will improve the chance of survival.

MARINE ACCIDENT INVESTIGATION BRANCH

Two fail to survive dinghy foundering

Narrative

At about 1130 on 16 December 1999, two men chose to take the *Samphire of Wells* on a short passage from Burnham Overy Staithe on the north Norfolk coast to the adjacent harbour of Wells-next-the-Sea. She was a 4.26m (14ft) open, clinker-built dinghy with a 10hp Yanmar diesel powered inboard engine.

It was a fine day, the sun was shining, it was high water and there was a light to moderate breeze. The total distance was about 6^{1}/$_{2}$ miles and both men had a working familiarity with small craft. The purpose of the passage was to take the dinghy to Wells for some touch-up work and a winter lay up. They had decided not to use road transport. Both men wore warm clothing and lifejackets but had no means of keeping water out in the event of immersion in the sea.

On the day before the passage was made a strong breeze to gale force onshore wind had been blowing. When the men failed to arrive at the expected time, initial concern developed into the realisation that something was wrong, and a full-scale search and rescue operation was launched. Shortly before 1900 that evening the body of one of the two occupants was found just outside Wells harbour wearing a fully inflated lifejacket. The body of the second man was discovered 6 days later, some 7 miles north of Cromer, and about 20 miles from

where the accident is thought to have occurred.

Although someone probably saw the dinghy while it was on passage, there were no witnesses to whatever happened and, apart from one or two items that have been recovered that probably came from the dinghy, there was no sign of the missing craft or its wreckage. It has not, therefore, been possible to determine the causes of the loss with any certainty. It is thought probable that the dinghy managed to cross the bar at the entrance to Burnham Overy Harbour, but may have shipped some water while doing so. The investigation has concluded that the most likely reason for the tragedy was that *Samphire of Wells* foundered at some stage while she was on passage between Burnham Overy Harbour and the entrance to Wells harbour. It did not require the addition of much water to capsize her, and it is thought that this is probably what happened.

Local sailing directions and knowledge warn users to be particularly careful when crossing specific harbour bars to one or two north Norfolk coast harbours and most especially when there is any northing in the wind. Evidence suggests that at least one of the victims would never knowingly take a risk if he perceived it to exist.

It is also thought that the benign conditions that prevailed in the shelter of the harbour gave a false sense of security, compared with the reality of disturbed water at the bar which may not have become apparent until the boat was committed.

The dinghy was entirely suitable for sheltered waters but vulnerable to swamping in rough seas.

Both men were wearing lifejackets but these failed to save them. It is probable that a combination of the cold, and seas breaking over them, led to them swallowing seawater to such an extent that they drowned. Neither man had any means of attracting attention once he was in the water.

157

The Lessons

1

Any passage, no matter how short or close inshore, is potentially dangerous if not properly prepared.

2

Preparations should include ensuring the craft is suitable for the planned passage and that the engine is sufficiently reliable. An infrequently used engine, or one that is not regularly maintained, is more likely to fail. Likewise, if its fuel has been left lying untouched in the storage tank for some time, the chances of moisture or other imperfections being present are much higher. This can affect engine performance. Other preparations should ensure that sufficient equipment is being carried for use in an emergency and should focus on improving the chances of survival and attracting attention.

3

Anybody planning a sea passage should check the weather forecast and, so far as possible, make an appraisal of recent conditions. Yesterday's weather can be a significant factor when determining today's sea state. It will also pay dividends to 'look over the sea wall' to observe the actual conditions. Very often the calm conditions of a sheltered harbour give way to something much stiffer once outside.

4

If you are unfamiliar with the waters to be sailed in, do not be shy about seeking the advice of someone with local knowledge. This is particularly pertinent if the intended passage involves crossing a bar.

5

A small dinghy is vulnerable to capsize if large quantities of water are shipped. Always carry a bailer and ensure it is attached to the craft in some way. If water comes on board, get rid of it as soon as possible.

6

Remember there are four factors involved in ensuring survival: keeping afloat, keeping warm, preventing the ingestion of seawater and attracting attention.

7

Lifejackets come in various forms. Make sure you are wearing the right type for the activity you are involved in; if in doubt seek professional help. Ensure it fits properly, has been serviced and is properly secured. Splash-proof hoods and crotch straps will do much to improve the chances of survival in rough seas.

8

Clothing should be suitable for the passage in question. Although nobody ever thinks they will be in a craft that founders, the risks escalate if you are in an open boat and making an open sea passage in winter. Cold water is often a primary cause of death or a major contributor to drowning. Consider wearing a dry suit with plenty of insulating clothing beneath it. Chest waders are unsuitable for wearing in small craft.

9

Give thought to how you might attract attention if you are left without any form of propulsion, or you find yourself alone in the sea.

10

Always inform a responsible and knowledge-able person or coastguard of your intentions, including your ETA, prior to departure and report your safe arrival on completion.

Footnote

This accident occurred in the middle of winter on a relatively isolated part of the coast with few people around. Had it been the summer or in an area where there was a greater chance of anything untoward being seen, the outcome might not have been so tragic. The lessons are nonetheless just as relevant.

158

Collision

I encountered my first collision at sea when I was just 16 years old. I had joined my first ship, a 6,000-tonne tramp ship, in London Docks, and after we sailed down the Thames we emerged into the English Channel. It was winter and even before we had dropped the pilot off at Dover we were in thick fog with the whistle blowing. This was a whole new experience for me, still wet behind the ears after leaving school just a couple of weeks before joining the ship.

This was back in 1950 when only a handful of ships were fitted with radar, and well before there was a traffic separation system in the Channel to provide one-way traffic lanes. So we chose the optimum course, heading for the turning point off Ushant. We were heading down Channel at a moderate speed when suddenly a ship appeared out of the fog right ahead. Fortunately it was an end-on meeting so there was a much-reduced chance of serious damage, but we certainly collided with a bang that reverberated throughout the boat. You could feel the ship heeling over but it was more of a glancing blow, bow to bow, that damaged the railings and bent a few plates, but nothing serious. It just made our hearts beat a bit faster.

Of course we all rushed out on deck to see what was happening and there was the other ship, similar in size, passing just a few feet away. We could almost reach out and shake hands with the crew. Then it disappeared into the fog just as quickly as it had arrived. A quick check showed no serious damage, but it was a salutary lesson and was my introduction to the possibility of disaster at sea.

M.V. MARJATA AT MELBOURNE

I joined the Marjata straight from school and the ship was in a collision just one day out from port on my first voyage.

Radar-assisted collision

Probably the most famous collision at sea was when the *Titanic* hit an iceberg back in 1912. Icebergs are the ultimate floating debris and will weigh more than the ship, so the ship always comes off worse. These days icebergs are carefully tracked as they drift south in the North Atlantic, and they also show up on radar, so ships are pretty safe, although the recent case of the cruise ship *Explorer* hitting ice in the Antarctic shows that the risk is still there. The risks are much higher for small craft operating among icebergs. A ship may shrug off a collision with the small ice, the bergy bits and growlers that come away from the main 'berg, but they are death to a small craft.

Another famous collision in the North Atlantic was that between the *Andrea Doria* and the *Stockholm*. These were both Atlantic liners and they were on opposing courses around the Nantucket Lightship. Both had radar, although back in 1956 when the collision occurred this was still a relatively new navigation tool. This collision has been hailed as the first 'radar-assisted collision', a term that was to be used in many more collisions, referring to the misuse of the information gained from the radar display. The fog was patchy and even though the two ships were in clear sight of each other when still a mile apart, the *Stockholm* tore into the side of the *Andrea Doria*, which capsized and sank. Forty-six people from the *Andrea Doria* and five from the *Stockholm* lost their lives. As the case was settled out of court, the blame for the collision was

never officially proportioned, but both ships contributed to the situation. This collision led to a close examination of the use of radar in collision avoidance, and the results set the pattern for future years.

These two ships should have been miles apart when they passed, but it shows how one ship, in trying to anticipate the movements of another, can compound a situation. As they had seen each other at a mile apart it should have been possible to avoid collision. But when ships travel at over 20 knots they close at the rate of nearly one mile every minute, and these are big ships that need time to change course and speed. It is interesting to see that in this collision, and in many more that have been analysed, at least one of the ships makes a turn almost at the last minute. The collision occurs when this turn is in the wrong direction, right across the bows of the other ship, suggesting that the other ship's course has been misinterpreted.

The collision between the cruise liner Norwegian Dream *and the container ship* Ever Decent *stunned the marine world. It was a collision that should never have happened.*

Shock and noise

That last minute before the collision must have seemed like an eternity to the watch-keepers on those two liners, but the die was already cast. Most collisions are quick and sudden. You never plan to hit anything, and while you might see another boat or ship just before you hit it, the first reaction to any collision is a great sense of shock. You cannot believe what has happened. You become rooted to the spot, not knowing what to do or how to cope, and the noise is incredible. The shock of a collision can last for several minutes, and those can be vital minutes if you want to save yourself and the boat.

A collision, whether it is with another ship or with floating debris of some sort, is likely to throw you across the boat. It is this and the dreadful noise that

A tanker shortly after being in collision with another ship. Here the damage was to the bow, which minimised the risk of oil pollution, one of the main concerns when ships are in collision.

alerts you to impending disaster. A collision in fog is probably worse because you do not see anything until the last moment. A recent collision in Boston Harbour between two ferries must have been terrifying for both passengers and crew. Although the ferries were damaged, no one on board was hurt, but the shock must have taken some time to wear off.

With small boats it is the suddenness of the collision that creates the shock. With ships it is different because their collisions seem to happen in slow motion. The ships involved are probably doomed when they are still half a mile or so apart. Either visually, or with radar, the crew can see what will happen. The next few minutes, when it is too late to take avoiding action, will be the longest of their lives. This interval occurs because large ships are not very manoeuvrable and must think in advance. Put the helm over in one of these ships and there is a considerable delay before anything starts to happen, and even when it does the turning is painfully slow. Try and make a crash stop, and the ship will travel a mile or two before it slows down appreciably.

Compare this with an immediately responsive boat where a crash stop can be a matter of seconds rather than minutes. Even if another craft looms out of the fog at close range, there should still be a good chance of avoiding it. It is this good manoeuvrability that accounts for the rarity of collisions between small craft. The statistics on collisions with fast ferries show over 1,000 reported incidents, with a considerable proportion of those occurring between two fast ferries. It makes you wonder what these so-called professional operators are doing, but it also highlights the increasing risk of high-speed operations. The statistics could be explained by the fact that ferry and ship collisions are always reported, whereas boat collisions may well be settled with a quick exchange of insurance details.

Two fast ferries collided off Macau harbour in 2006, but fortunately without any loss of life or injury. The 28m monohull *Dong Qu Yi* was left sinking with only the bow above water, while the 48m *New World LXXXV* was only slightly damaged. Fast ferry operations require a high-calibre watchkeeper, because things happen very quickly at high speed. Although two miles from another ship, at 40 knots you'll reach it in under a minute and a half, which does not allow a lot of time for altering course or speed. Factor in the added complications of poor visibility and having to keep to a tight operating schedule, and you have a potential for disaster that will be exacerbated by the high speeds involved. I am convinced that many ferry collisions occur in poor visibility, when the ferries are trying to keep to a schedule and are reluctant to slow down.

Contact with whales

Another collision danger for fast ferries is making contact with whales. There has been an increasing number of these in recent years, perhaps raised by an increase in reporting, but also by the rapid increase in fast ferry operations. We were not far out of New York on *Virgin Atlantic Challenger,* making our record crossing, when a whale surfaced close ahead. When you sight a whale like this there is no indication of the direction in which it is heading, but thankfully it passed safely down the side of the boat. It was close enough to smell and when you can smell a whale you know you are too close. Contact would have done neither of us any good as we were travelling at 50 knots.

Harbours

There is always the risk of injury in a collision and there does seem to be a growing number of collisions between small boats where injury or death results. You can't laugh these off, and they seem to be prevalent at night in harbours. I have little doubt in my mind that yacht tenders and similar craft running at night without lights are a major worry, and given the time of day, alcohol will often be a contributory factor. Even if the small boats have lights it is not always easy to see them against shore lights. I came across an unlit boat one evening when returning across a harbour, and at first there did not appear to be anyone on board. Closer inspection revealed a white backside going up and down in the bottom of the boat. The boat was drifting up the harbour in the dark, while the couple were otherwise engaged.

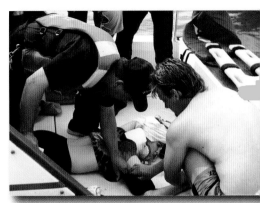

Caring for survivors after a collision involving powerboats.

Speed is another factor in harbour collisions. I know of one case where a RIB running at around 20 knots ran into a ferry at night. The ferry was big enough, but unless you are aware and alert, it is not always easy to see something moving slowly against the shore lights. The ferry shrugged off the incident, and the RIB came off worse. With its sudden stop against the hull of the ferry, the crew were catapulted overboard against the side of the ferry and seriously injured. In another case, one boat ran right over the top of another in a British harbour, resulting in the death of one crewmember. This is the sort of collision that may lead to changes in the regulations by which we operate boats in harbours. I am not convinced that regulations will improve the situation, but it is really the only weapon that the authorities have when trying to enforce moderation in boat driving.

Compared with the USA, there are relatively few collision incidents in European waters involving fast boats. In one accident in Florida, a 45ft Sonic high-performance sports boat sliced through a cabin cruiser on the Intracoastal Canal in the dark, killing all six people on the cruiser. Wreckage was reported as being spread for nearly half a mile over the water and a man and woman on board the Sonic were thrown out, while the boat continued at speed before hitting a dock on the waterway. These two were rescued but taken to hospital in critical condition. The Sonic was reported as being capable of 80mph, but it was not known how fast it was going at the time of the collision. There was a 25mph limit in force on that stretch of the waterway, but the disintegration of the cabin cruiser suggests the Sonic was travelling at considerable speed. Alcohol is suspected of being a contributory cause in this accident. The Sonic driver was convicted of manslaughter and sentenced to 85 years in prison. Finding proof in this sort of case can be difficult, but here there seemed to be little doubt.

Recording collisions

If you trawl the Internet for boating accidents, America comes up time and time again. America probably has the most crowded waters in the world as far as leisure boating is concerned, with over 17 million registered boats, so you could argue that collisions are almost inevitable. The statistics show that collisions

Good clear navigation lights are essential to prevent collisions at night, but the flag on this motor yacht is covering the stern light.

are at the top of the table as far as accident causes are concerned with over 2,500 per year, and that is just collisions with other vessels. If you add in collisions with objects then this increases by another 1,000. It is not hard to see why there are so many marine lawyers in the US.

One embarrassing collision occurred when a Florida Fish and Wildlife patrol boat collided with a manatee. Manatees are a protected species, and the patrol boat was out there to monitor the speed of other boaters to limit collisions with these gentle animals. The officer on board said that he was accelerating after leaving a manatee zone when the collision occurred. The wildlife people said they got some useful information from the collision that could be used for more effective regulations and possible new vessel designs for the future.

Any boat that comes to a stop very quickly is going to cause injury to the people on board. I do a lot of expert witness work investigating accidents involving boats and their occupants, and most of these involve injury. I am always amazed at the stories people come up with after they have been involved in an accident, but then I guess the same thing happens with car accidents. The Marine Accident Investigation Branch is the official body that investigates marine accidents involving death or injury in Britain, and there are examples of their reports at the end of each chapter in this book.

Colregs

There is no doubt that if collision regulations (Colregs) are followed to the letter, then collisions should not occur. Running at night without lights is forbidden, as is running at speed in poor visibility, and operating at night in a crowded harbour is certainly against the spirit of the rules. However, even some of the most basic rules are commonly ignored. I have seen a fast boat approaching on my port bow, and when we were nearby it became obvious that he had no intention of giving way (assuming that there was someone at the helm at the time). I managed to take avoiding action but things got very close.

A commercial vessel skipper recently said that he could only apply the collision regulations in a close-quarters situation if he knew that the other vessel or vessels knew and understood them as well. There is just no way of finding out until it is almost too late, so you have to play it defensively. Trying to avoid any close-quarters situation is the safest solution of all. There is no point in being right and dead. As one ship's captain said, 'The proper conduct of seamanship is to make allowances for the unseamanlike conduct of others.'

Common sense demands that you act defensively in a potential collision situation and that particularly applies when ships and boats are mixing in the same waterway. You can be a small boat in a very big ocean and have no guarantee that a big ship has seen you, and even if he has there is no guarantee that he will take avoiding action. Might is right in these situations, and I can't help feeling that in most ship/boat encounters it will be the ship coming up astern of the boat that is the real danger. How many people on watch on a small boat take the trouble to look astern? The problem here is that on many boats it is very difficult to see astern as there is no view from the helm. A lot of ships these days travel at a considerable speed: 20, 25 or even 30 knots. So even if you are in a planing boat cruising at 25 knots there could still be a ship coming up behind you, and at night your low stern light will be little more than a glow-worm on his horizon and your vessel a tiny speck on his radar. With some of the modern fast ferries travelling at 40 knots, a yacht under sail could be hard pushed to get out of the way even if he tried because there is simply no time. If you sight the ferry three miles away you will have barely four minutes to take avoiding action!

Small boats at night

At night the stern light of a small boat can be very hard to see even when it is the correct size and brightness as required by the regulations. It might look bright when you are close to it but from a distance it can be very hard to pick out and it is very difficult to judge your distance off from a single white light at night. The regulations require the light to be visible from a distance of two miles, and most probably are, but the chances of it being picked up from the bridge of a ship at that range will be very small. The stern light is usually quite low and that can make it disappear from view when the boat is going up and down in waves. To make matters worse some boats have a flag at the stern that can obstruct the light.

I don't know why there is such reluctance among boaters to have the brightest possible light at the stern, because that bright light could mean the difference between life and death. There was a time when battery power was a problem on sailboats and some sailors were reluctant to drain precious resources with powerful bright lights. But on modern yachts, electrical power is much less of a problem. Perhaps the time has come to change the rules, to have something more distinctive as a stern light so that there is a better chance of it being seen.

Yacht builders need to think a lot more carefully about the navigational lights they install and where they install them. I have come across boats where the masthead light and the stern lights have been transposed and others where the lights can be blocked by people standing at the helm. Sailboat lights in particular can be hard to see and identify when they are at the top of the mast, and the situation is not helped by having red and green lights rather than the brighter white. It is folly to think that you are safe because you can see other vessels at night, because they need to be able to see you as well. The only way to ensure this is to have lights that do their job.

AIS

Electronics may be able to come to the rescue in the quest to make yachts more 'visible' to shipping. Radar reflectors can make yachts more 'radar visible', and there are radar transponders that are electrically powered and send out a return signal when triggered by a radar beam. These help to enhance the radar image of a yacht, but the biggest hope for making yachts visible is the AIS (Automatic Identification System). AIS is an active system where details of a ship, its course and speed, its destination and many other details are sent out automatically by a VHF radio link. These signals are picked up by other ships and can be automatically plotted on an electronic chart. This means that there is a positive identification of a

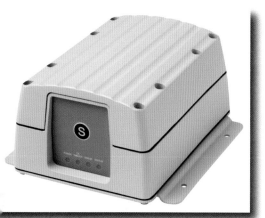

AIS units could be a very valuable means of allowing small craft to show up on the radar of big ships but the ships have the option of switching out the small boat units if there are too many of them.

target which, unlike radar, is limited only by the VHF radio range. AIS is a mandatory fitting on ships, and now there is a Class B AIS available at relatively low cost for yachts.

In theory this should be salvation for yachts entering shipping channels because it means that they can be positively identified at considerable range, certainly from five miles away. Ships will pick up the AIS signal in plenty of time to take any necessary action and yachts will also have a positive identification of other craft around them. This should be the safety system that everybody has been waiting for, and a chance to greatly reduce the risk of collision at sea. Unfortunately, however, this is not the case. Because of the fear that hundreds of yachts fitted with AIS would swamp the displays on board the ships that use what is known as Class A AIS, most modern Class A AIS units have been fitted with a switch that enables all the Class B signals to be removed from the display. It must be wonderful for a ship that is operating in crowded waters to simply remove a whole host of the targets from the display, simply by flicking a switch. So what appeared to be a potentially great safety system for yachts actually offers no guarantees at all. It really is a mess out there and all the signs suggest that things are getting worse, not better.

Changes to Colregs

A proposal being put to the International Maritime Organisation (IMO) seeks to change the Colregs in quite a dramatic way. Put simply, this proposal would change the rules so that all leisure craft under 20m have to give way to all commercial craft. Some would argue that this is what happens now in practice. While that basic rule change sounds a good idea, it throws up many problems. First you have to be able to identify what is a commercial vessel and what is a leisure craft. The proposal aims to get round this by insisting that all leisure craft have a red and white cylinder shape at their masthead in daylight. At night they would have a light showing a quick burst of flashes every two minutes and a dedicated sound signal. To someone sitting behind an office desk these proposals might sound rational but to the practical seaman at sea they just won't work.

Imagine what the sailing fraternity would think about having to display a large red and white cylinder at the masthead. It is not exactly going to improve the sailing performance of the yacht, quite apart from the problem of actually finding some method of securing it. It is very hard to judge the distance of a rapidly flashing white light, and what would happen in crowded waters with many of these lights flashing away? Then you need to define which vessels are leisure craft. Is a yacht that is under charter a commercial or a leisure craft? What about sailing dinghies? Would a large red and white cylinder compromise their sailing or even capsize the boat? There are many small craft around that could not comply, but this proposal is a sign that people are thinking and certainly I can see changes on the horizon. It seems to me that if such a problem exists then segregation would be a better solution than complex rules that nobody is likely to follow.

It is hard to find good statistics, but when reading reports of collisions at sea there seem to be many more between commercial vessels than there are involving leisure craft. In the MAIB reports there appear to be more collisions between ships and fishing boats than there ever are between ships and leisure craft. In Italy there were 65 reported contacts between commercial and leisure craft over a five-year period and most of those occurred in harbour where everybody is much closer together. Most harbour authorities already have powers to impose some form of segregation between small and large craft, and indeed the Colregs give ships in narrow channels some priority anyway, so the means to solve this problem already exist. If leisure is to give way to commercial as proposed, the assumption is that the leisure craft actually has the means and the time to keep out of the way. With fast ferries doing 40 or more knots and a yacht doing perhaps 5-knots there may not be time.

Dover Straits

To a certain extent, leisure does give way to commercial in the crowded waters of the Dover Straits. This has been achieved by the creation of the Traffic Separation Scheme. This routes south-west-going ships into one channel and north-west-going ships into another, while leaving the inshore sea areas for small craft. However, in the eyes of IMO, small craft allowed to use these inshore lanes must be under 20m in length; anything over this size has to mix it with the big ships. I am sure that most small craft skippers, even in sizes up to 30m or more, would prefer to be away from the big ships and not be forced into close quarters with them.

The Coastguard monitors the Dover Straits with radar but this is mainly to identify the cause of accidents or transgressions of the rules rather than to prevent collisions.

The Traffic Separation Scheme in the Dover Straits was a pioneering system introduced in the early 1970s, that is now followed in many parts of the world. It was initiated when a collision occurred between a 10,000 tonne Cypriot cargo ship and the tanker *Texaco Caribbean*. The cargo ship was badly damaged and was towed away for repairs. However, the tanker exploded and broke in two, with the loss of eight lives. The following day, the cargo ship Brandenburg hit the wreckage of the tanker and capsized and sank, with the loss of 21 crewmembers. Six weeks later a Greek cargo ship hit the wreckage and sank with no survivors, bringing the total lives lost to 51.

The initial collisions took place in fog, and I was out there on a Trinity House ship trying to lay marker buoys on the wrecks. It was still thick fog and was one of the most frightening jobs of my life, with ships appearing just a few hundred feet away, running at full speed and only just managing to miss us and the wrecks, despite broadcast warnings. It took six years after that incident for the Traffic Separation Scheme to come into effect, which shows how slow the IMO is when it comes to changing the Colregs to accommodate changing circumstances. There was a repeat performance of this incident in 2002 when the *Kariba* collided with the large car carrier *Tricolor*. The *Tricolor* sank and the following night a German ship hit the submerged hull and spent seven hours perched on top of it until she was towed off as the tide rose.

167

Despite this incident the separation scheme has certainly worked to reduce collisions in the Dover Straits, and in many other parts of the world, but I cannot help feeling that the situation is becoming critical again. The reason now is not so much the shipping going up and down the Channel, but the ferries going across it. There are reckoned to be over 400 ships a day going through the Dover Straits and up to 250 per day going across it. That is a lot of traffic. Some of the ships using the Straits may be 320m container ships doing 23 or 24 knots and the ferries are running at over 20 knots and possibly carrying over 2,000 or more passengers.

The ferries have introduced their own one-way system across the Channel, but that is mainly so that they do not collide with each other. They still have to find a way through the streams of ships passing through the Straits, and to do this they give way to everything. The Colregs allow this as long as it is done early in any encounter so when a ferry leaves Dover it gets up to speed and then looks for a gap through the shipping using radar to calculate passing distances or potential meeting points. The ferries plan never to pass less than one mile from the crossing ships, and when the system works and the crossing ships maintain course and speed, then everything is fine. However, the margins are small and it will only take a technical failure on one ship to quickly open up the possibility of collision. What happens if the ferry radar stops working or is faulty? And what happens if one of the crossing ships loses power and slows dramatically in the path of the ferry? What happens if the ferry watch officer makes a wrong assessment of the collision situation? The margins are just too small for comfort and I am convinced that catastrophe is inevitable. Already there are many near misses every day. Imagine the situation when a ferry with 2,000 passengers on board collides with a tanker carrying highly inflammable liquids. Perhaps you can see why I am a great fan of the Channel Tunnel.

In making their collision risk assessment, the ferries seem to take little account of any small craft that may be passing through the Straits. Apparently the Coastguard, who maintain a watch on the Straits, cannot pick up yachts on their surveillance radar either. So you really take your life in your hands if your passage carries you anywhere near the entrance to Dover Harbour in a small craft. The ferry officers have a full-time job trying to negotiate the crossing ships situation as they leave harbour, without being concerned by passing yachts. The Dover Straits are a bit like nautical Russian roulette, with the gun loaded heavily against small craft!

Collisions in fog

In fog the situation is even more dire. The ship will have radar but there is no guarantee that a small craft is going to show up, particularly if there is a sea running and lots of sea clutter around the centre of the radar display. If you have radar on board the small craft, then you'll have a good chance of seeing the ships. Even then, taking avoiding action is not always easy and there have been several reports of yachts conforming to the Colregs, but still the other ships kept bearing down. It can take some time to work out whether that approaching ship is on a

There is very little time for collision avoidance in fog once visual contact is made. This is why the use of radar is so important.

collision course, and if it is a fast ship you may only have a few minutes to decide what to do. The situation gets more complex when in crowded waters and you may have to deal with more than one ship.

To put this situation into perspective, the Dover Straits are the busiest shipping lanes in the world. The actions of the ships are governed by the Collision Regulations, but probably only 40% of the ships follow these regulations as they should, and about one-third of the ships using the Straits have made up their own rules, and not informed the others. One half of the Straits are monitored by the French and the other half by the British, but neither have any powers of enforcement. Shipping does not slow down in fog and does not sound fog signals as required by regulations; they rely on seeing other vessels on their radar and if you don't show, you don't exist. Amazingly there are relatively few incidents, but the considerable number of near misses should serve as an early warning sign.

Just to add to the problems for small craft in fog, very few ships sound their fog signals, even though it is still mandatory to do so. I have been on a cross-Channel ferry in thick fog and not only were there no fog signals being sounded, but the ship did not slow down either and proceeded at over 20 knots when visibility was little more than the ship's length. The navigators would argue that they can 'see' other ships on their radar and they are skilled enough to take the necessary avoiding action, but pity the small craft without radar that might get in their way.

In the case of the yacht *Ouzo* heading down Channel from the Isle of Wight, the three-man crew were lost in a collision or near miss with a ship. This highlights the risks involved in any meeting between small craft and shipping. While the full facts of this case have not been identified, it seems highly likely that the yacht was hit by a ship, probably a ferry.

In any situation involving a ship and a small craft it will always be the small craft that will come off worse, and the chances are there will be no survivors to tell the story. Bodies may turn up shortly afterwards, but the craft itself will usually sink without trace and the disappearance of the yacht is only likely to be reported some time after it is overdue. In the case of the *Ouzo*, the bodies of the crew were found not long after the collision, and it was reckoned that one had remained alive for up to 12 hours in the water. However, the ship did not report the collision, so no search was started until the yacht was reported overdue.

The ferry **Pride of Bilboa** *was thought to have been the ship that collided with the yacht* **Ouzo**, *resulting in the deaths of the three-man crew.*

This collision occurred in the waters off Singapore, which are one of several collision risk hot spots around the world.

Narrow channels

A similar situation is developing in the Bosphorus Straits in Turkey. This narrow twisting channel is open to international shipping and around 1,350 ships pass through each day. There are also reckoned to be 2,000 ferry crossings every day. The Straits house a dense population along the banks; the channel has four acute bends, and in places is only 700m wide with considerable currents. This is probably the most challenging shipping channel in the world, and although the traffic control system has helped the Bosphorus, it makes the Dover Straits look like a picnic in the park. With the channel being used increasingly for the shipping of oil cargoes out from Russia and the Ukraine, the potential for disaster is enormous and very worrying. The obvious solution is a pipeline to bypass the Straits. In 1994 the tanker *Nassia* was in collision; it ended up drifting and burning for a week before the situation was brought under control. A traffic control system has reduced the number of collisions, and the majority of disasters that occur here are now groundings.

More losses and near misses

In 2000 a Twister-class yacht set sail from Ijmuiden in Holland bound for Harwich, but never arrived. Three weeks after the yacht disappeared three bodies were washed up on the Dutch coast. The fourth body was found three months later and the wreck of the yacht was trawled up a month after that. The skipper was an experienced yachtsman, but he had a novice crew who were students from Cambridge University. Apparently, the skipper left one or more of the inexperienced crew on watch, while he slept. An earlier crew had reported some near misses on the trip across to Holland. It can only be speculated that there was a collision but the wreckage revealed no firm evidence.

The yacht *Bluebell of Warsash* collided with a ship in mid-Channel in 1999, and lived to tell the tale. They had no radar on board, but they sighted a brightly illuminated ferry ahead on a near reciprocal course. They reckoned that it would pass clear down the starboard side, but there was another ship on a crossing course on the starboard side. This ship passed ahead of the ferry and then closed the yacht very quickly, possibly having altered course to avoid the ferry. The bulbous bow of the ship hit the yacht, but it was a glancing blow and the yacht survived with one man overboard. After investigation the ship was blamed for the accident. The yacht received only superficial damage, but it must have been a very scary incident; the crew were lucky to get away so lightly.

As you might expect, near misses are much more frequent than actual collisions, and most reported incidents occur in crowded waters. In one case a yacht only missed the Southampton to Cowes ferry by a matter of a few metres. It is scary out there, and if you've ever been very close to a big ship at sea it is not an experience that you will want to repeat. I have done so twice, when the ship was trying to rescue us, and you almost feel that you would rather not be rescued than get that close to a ship. They look enormous when close by and taking defensive action is always the best tactic, provided you have room for the manoeuvre and keep your distance.

Who is to blame in these ship/yacht encounters? Each case has to be looked at individually of course, and it is easy to blame the ship because it failed to keep a good lookout and did not see the yacht. However, it takes two to have a collision and anyone in a small craft operating in the shipping lanes needs to navigate defensively. First, try to avoid mixing with the big ships, and second, keep a good look out, particularly astern. In a small craft you should never assume that the ship has seen you. It is interesting to note that most of the reported encounters between ships and small craft involved sail rather than powerboats, and I can't help wondering if this is because they think that power has to give way to sail; or perhaps it is because there is a reluctance to give up hard-won distance to windward, to pass clear of a closing ship; or perhaps a boat under sail loses control when the wind disappears in the lee of a big ship. Each incident will be different and in a collision it is rare for just one party to take all the blame. Remember that, if it avoids a collision, the Colregs allow you to take action even if you are the stand-on vessel.

Stowaway?

Collisions can have their humorous side. Take the case of the lone yachtsman in his 10m sailboat off the west coast of Florida. It was about 05:00 when his yacht was in collision with a tug towing a barge. The yacht was seriously damaged in the collision and drifted back towards the barge. The yachtsman managed to jump onto the unmanned barge and it was about five hours later that the tug crew, who were unaware of the collision, saw the man on the deck of the barge. It was immediately suspected that he was a stowaway, so a joint Coastguard and Customs team were called out to board the barge and capture him. He was held in handcuffs until his story had been confirmed and at that point his status changed from stowaway to survivor and he was landed ashore. A lucky escape in more ways than one.

Then there was the case of the two fishing boats that collided in the middle of the ocean. Fishing boats are one of the few types of vessel that actually work at sea, so in addition to doing the navigating they are busy hauling and sorting the catch. It is not hard to imagine that the business of keeping a lookout can take second place to the many other tasks on hand. However, these two boats collided because the skipper of one was sitting on the wheelhouse deck stripping down the echo sounder to try to fix it. There was not a lot of point in fixing the echo sounder if the boat was going to sink in a collision. It sounds amusing but collisions are never really funny. They are out-of-control situations and all a seaman wants to do is turn the clock back a minute or two, and do that bit over again.

Most of the collisions between yachts and ships seem to occur at night and darkness certainly puts a different perspective on things, particularly if you are not used to sailing at night. In clear weather you should see a ship's lights some way off, but it is not always easy to judge distances. It is often when the ship gets close that you may lose sight of its lights, or you find yourself looking at the horizon when really you should be looking up.

I found out about this problem when I was crossing the Channel in fog many years ago. I was on a small 1,000 tonne ship; in those days we had no radar and, of course, there was thick fog. We were blowing the foghorn and we heard a deep-throated fog signal in the distance. It was the recognisable foghorn of the big Atlantic liners that were still running in those days. Slowing down we peered into the fog as the fog signal was getting louder and louder and still we could not see anything. The other ship was now so close that its fog signal was making our ship vibrate and we stopped, thinking we were going to get run over at any minute. It was pitch black out there, with not a light to be seen, and then suddenly we looked up and there were the lights of the other ship passing close above us. It was the ocean liner *Queen Mary*, and she was so big that we had to look upwards to see the lights. That was one scary moment.

The *Queen Mary* frightened us, but in 1942 she had a much more serious incident when she collided with her escorting cruiser, HMS *Curacao,* about 20 miles off the Irish coast. The *Queen Mary* sliced the *Curacao* in two with the loss of over 300 lives, but she could not stop to help because it would have put her at risk from the U-Boats in the area. Only her high speed made her safe.

Submarines and other debris

There have been a number of reported collisions between ships and submarines. You might expect the submarine to come off worse in these incidents, but in many cases, particularly those involving fishing boats, there is no clear proof. The French trawler *Bugaled Breizh* mysteriously sank south of the British coast in 2007. A French judge investigating the incident overruled the French marine investors' conclusion that the most likely cause of the loss was the trawl snagging on the seabed, and suggested instead that collision with a submarine was most likely. It was a more clear-cut case when another French trawler was rammed and sunk in the English Channel. Traces of paint on a Turkish ship confirmed that she was the culprit, but she had not stopped and had continued her voyage. It is hard to believe that this can happen but it does, often

These two ships were in collision in the River Schelde in Belgium. Ships operate at much closer margins in rivers and harbours so the risk of collision in considerably increased.

with the culprit hoping to get away with it. In a collision in Hong Kong between two container ships, the MSC *Ilona* and the *Hyundai Advance,* the latter ship tried to 'escape' the consequences, but was stopped by Chinese patrol boats.

Collisions with other craft are a problem that should be avoidable, but colliding with floating debris is just a question of luck. You would think from the number of reports about yachts hitting debris or whales that the oceans were littered with them. I have travelled thousands of miles at sea, much of it at high speed when debris could be a major threat, and yet I have never been involved in a collision with debris and have only ever seen something that appeared dangerous on a couple of occasions, both close inshore. This makes me wonder about many of these so-called collisions, and whether the reported incident was a cover up for some form of structural failure in the hull.

As far as your insurance company is concerned it is much easier to blame a sinking at sea on hitting debris than to suggest that it was a structural failure in the hull. The chances are that a structural failure would make the insurance null and void so what better way to get out of it than by saying you hit something. Sure, there are lots of shipping containers that get washed overboard in storms due to lashing failures, but it is my guess that most of these would sink pretty rapidly before they became a danger to small craft. If the containers do not sink then why don't we find them washed up on beaches? Another factor is that most of the reported collisions with debris appear to occur in ocean waters rather than inshore, which is where you expect to find debris.

Another interesting factor is that a surprising number of the incidents involving debris strikes seem to occur to multi-hulls. Call me cynical if you like, but I would suggest that multi-hulls are more prone to structural failures than a monohull, which could explain the higher percentage of multi-hulls that report striking debris.

There also appears to be a higher percentage of competition sailing yachts experiencing debris strikes than cruising yachts. Under competition conditions the speeds are almost certainly going to be higher, but

173

To try to discover what happens when fast powerboats collide, a series of collisions between unmanned boats was staged in the US.

it would be good to think that the pace would also be matched by a higher level of focus and concentration, which ought to detect floating debris before contact. The higher speeds would certainly mean that any contact with debris would have more serious consequences, and of course there are also a lot of single-handers reporting debris strikes, where the level of lookout would be reduced. Competition yachts tend to be built as light as possible so there is also an increased possibility of hull failure, particularly around the keel area, and this could lead to a higher percentage of structural failures.

I would expect a higher level of debris to be found in coastal waters, where trees and other items have been washed out from rivers and harbours. The only serious debris I have ever seen was a 90ft long steel pole some 3ft in diameter that was initially reported as a small submarine floating in the Thames Estuary. I was working for Trinity House at the time on their lighthouse tenders and it was our job to find and remove this object. Any ship or boat hitting it could have been in serious trouble, but despite floating in busy shipping lanes there were no reports of any damage.

Powerboats perhaps have the edge over sailboats when it comes to hitting debris; at least the planing type do. Any powerboat that hits something floating just awash would be likely to ride up over the debris rather than impact directly with it, provided that the boat was on the plane. Of course any collision of this nature is likely to cause serious damage to the stern gear, so it will not be a minor incident. Unless the stern gear is completely ripped out, the hull should stay intact despite the high speed of collision. Again there are very few reports of these and you almost never hear of hull structural failures in powerboats.

Competition can produce its own problems with collisions, and there is probably a higher percentage of collisions between racing boats, both power and sail, than from any other cause. Sailboats in particular are very vulnerable at a start, because this will be when they are heading into wind and tacking and still be at very close quarters. It does not require much of an error of judgement for two boats to collide in this situation, and judging by the shouting that takes place near misses are frequent.

Powerboats

Powerboats that are racing should all be heading in the same direction, but at very high speeds they are more vulnerable to colliding with spectator boats. At 100mph it only takes a small dinghy to come out from behind another boat for a near miss, and I have seen it happen many times when I was racing. Today, organisers have taken steps to ensure that courses are patrolled and kept clear. Racing powerboats are particularly vulnerable on a turn mark, when one might spin out and another run over the top of it.

Any close-quarters situation with boats and ships is a potential collision risk area and it is terrifying to see the risks that people take when they are trying to get close enough to get good photos. I have over 60 years' experience of working with boats and ships, and this has given me a lot of experience of disasters, but it never fully prepares you for the shock of sudden collision at sea. Disasters at sea come in two forms: the slowly evolving disaster such as the boat slowly sinking or the weather steadily deteriorating, and the sudden disaster such as a collision or grounding.

Overrun by a Cat

One collision I was involved in was a near-death experience; probably the closest call I have ever had on the water and the shock was intense. Even after all these years I still find myself shaking when I think about it. It all started quite innocently. We were out on a photo shoot, taking pictures of a brand new 65ft, 35 knot power catamaran. Back in the 1990s power catamarans of this size and speed were still a novelty, so we wanted to get some really dramatic close-up pictures. Manoeuvring around and trying for dramatic angles put us in the wrong place at the wrong time. It was the first and only time that I have actually been hit by another boat, and I can assure you it is a very painful experience.

The photograph I took moments before this fast catamaran hit us in what was a near death experience.

Our camera platform was a 40ft sailing cat, a nice stable base for photography. The plan was for us to motor at a steady pace along this river, where there were no speed limits, and let the power cat manoeuvre around us. I wanted to get some 'wow' pictures looking down the tunnel of the power cat, so we asked the driver to come up astern of us and then peel off to one side at the last minute. That sounded pretty straightforward and it was well within the manoeuvring capabilities of the power cat.

The pictures were looking great through the camera viewfinder and I kept clicking away as it got closer and closer, totally focused on the view. I wasn't really monitoring the progress of the power cat, just concentrating on getting those good photos. The next thing I knew, or at least can remember, was being hit by the boat we were photographing. It was a really heavy blow, hard enough to knock me flat onto the deck, which was just as well because the boat kept on coming. It climbed right over the sailing cat, and only stopped when it hit the mast!

I was lying on the deck still clutching my camera; it must have been the stanchions that had stopped me being knocked overboard. I was in a state of considerable shock and I couldn't understand what had happened. It was all so sudden, and I was down, lying on the deck with the vee of the power cat's hull just inches above my nose. The keel of that hull had carved a groove into the deck just two feet to the side of me, just a few inches more to one side and it would have gone over me. It was all too quick to be scared (that would come later) but I can still see that hull with its red anti-fouling just inches above my head. Thank God I didn't put my arms out, otherwise I might have had trouble writing this story.

The noise was incredible and it seemed to go on for ever, finally quieting down so that there was just the final tinkle from some stainless steel tubing that had been dislodged in the collision. Then temporary peace, until the power cat started to slide backwards off the top of our boat. Again, the noise was incredible. Then peace once more. I did not want to move – I was frightened of what I might see in the cockpit, fearing the dead and mangled bodies of the other guys on board. Then I saw movement and by some miracle, none of the three of us on board was seriously hurt.

Training and seamanship took over. When I got to my feet I was hurting all over, but I remember being much more concerned about the boat. After such a collision it must be leaking or even sinking. We checked the bilges and they were dry. We checked the steering and that still worked although the steering wheel was rather an odd shape, having gone up the tunnel. The mast and rigging were a bit bent and buckled but the engine was still running so it was time to turn round and head for home to sort things out.

The power cat was fine and there was no apparent damage at all so we all headed back to the marina to find out what had happened. It turned out that because it was a new boat, the driver was learning about its handling as he went along. He was focusing on coming up astern of us at speed, and then at the critical moment he hesitated, unsure of which way to turn. By the time he had made up his mind it was too late. The power cat had water jet propulsion and even at that late moment these jets would have had enough braking power to stop the boat, if only he had used the jet reverse control instead of the throttles. Yes, the throttles would slow the boat, but only in a leisurely fashion and so this big planing catamaran just kept on coming and ran over us.

I have a hazy recollection of making my way home by train (I was in no fit state to drive). By now the shaking had started and I could not think straight or even focus on anything. I was like that for three days before the shock started to wear off. I was also black and blue all over with the bruising from the impact, but I kept on telling myself that it was better than being dead.

High-speed craft

I had a stark reminder of that collision when I was in Singapore, training their Coastguard in boat interception techniques. The Coastguard there has a need to be able to stop high-speed boats at sea and, apart from firing guns, the only way to do it is to power in alongside and pin the two boats together. It takes determination and courage to do this at 50 knots in the dark but it can be a very effective way of stopping the bad guys. Those were intentional collisions and it was pretty exciting stuff, but you already know when doing that sort of manoeuvre that the risks are great. We were as prepared for them as you can be.

High-speed craft on the water have only really appeared over the past 20 years. It is over that period that the numbers and the size of the fast craft have increased dramatically, and the advent of the fast ferry has added a whole new dimension to the risks of collision at sea. In terms of quantity these fast ferries are still relatively rare, but the impact they have on collision risk is out of all proportion to their numbers. Statistics suggest that there have been over 1,000 collisions involving these craft, which is very high when you consider that there are probably only around 2,000 of them roaming the oceans. It is not just fast ferries that present this problem because there are an increasing number of leisure boats that can travel at over 30 knots, and they are more likely to be operated by people with less experience.

Congested space

A number of collisions involving high-speed craft have occurred around Hong Kong, where numerous fast ferries criss-cross the crowded waters close alongside a wide variety of other craft. It is the same in Bangkok, and I have a strong recollection of looking down from my hotel room there and watching the chaos of the traffic on the river below. You wonder why there are no collisions, but in reality they probably occur quite frequently. Here it is size and speed that rule the situation. The commuter ferries that ply the regular routes up and down the river run at over 30 knots and seem to employ a breed of driver specially trained in aggression. Speed is king on the Chaophraya River and the faster you go, it seems,

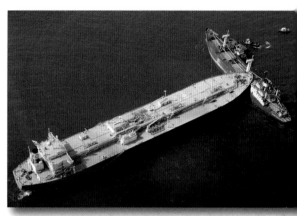

A T-Bone collision that would appear to be a serious case of misjudgement.

the higher priority you have. So the slow ferries that cross the river tread a tentative course, weaving between the faster traffic, which uses its strident horns to demand right of way.

There are no speed limits. Twice a day the Coastguard patrol boat cruises up and down the river at a leisurely pace, but it is a token gesture. There are no rules of the road, and it is survival of the fittest. The commuter ferries with their graceful swan-neck bows fight for space at the landing stages. The long tail boats know their place and sneak in when there is a gap, and somehow the cross-river ferries find a space. Passengers have to be quick: the ferries only stay alongside for 20 seconds or so and marshals with portable loudhailers harangue the crowds to jump in quickly. It looks like organised chaos, but it works. Is this the way forward for collision avoidance? It seems to work in Bangkok, so could it work in the wider world? The Chaophraya River looks rather like the Dover Straits in miniature and the same attitudes seem to prevail there.

What is the answer?

Closer to home, the fast-ferry traffic across the English Channel is developing into something of a nightmare free-for-all situation for small craft. In order to ensure their survival, so the ferries say, they ignore the Colregs and give way to everything on the water, whether they have right of way or not. Their system is to put what you might call a bubble around every ship on the radar, this bubble extending one mile ahead of the ship and half a mile at the sides and stern. This represents the no-go area that the ferry must not enter to ensure a safe passage and is aimed at making sure that there is adequate clearance from the passing ships. When questioned, they are a bit vague about whether the privilege of having this safety bubble extends to any small craft that might be using the shipping lanes. I hope so, because every vessel over 20m has to use these lanes, and so is vulnerable to the crossing ferries.

This ferry system has worked so far and the only collisions recorded have been between two ferries, one high-speed and one conventional, and that was close to the entrance to Dover in poor visibility. The ferry people say they need to adopt this system because they cannot trust the shipping going up and

Collisions can sometimes result in a total loss.

down the Channel to take the action required of them under the Colregs. There is a misconception among regular ship navigators that if they are in the traffic lanes then they have priority over the crossing traffic, just as they think they have priority over small craft, but this is not the case. It is a major accident waiting to happen, particularly when nobody seems to be prepared to slow down in fog these days.

This problem with cross-Channel ferries is repeated on a smaller scale in many parts of the world. By their very nature, ferries tend to be going across shipping channels because they link the two sides of a channel through which ships pass. If everyone follows the rules, then all should be well, but often they do not and it is small wonder that collisions do occur. One of the reasons for this is that while ferries may be familiar and comfortable with close-quarters situations, normal shipping is not and this can lead to unpredictable action. There was a serious collision in the Messina Straits (between Italy and Sicily), in 2007 when a cargo ship ran into a high-speed ferry. The rights and wrongs of the case are still being argued, but the cargo ship carved a great gash in the side of the ferry, and the bow of the ship went right into the bridge, killing the captain and three crew and injuring over 100 passengers. Reports suggest that a third ship was involved in the manoeuvres that led up to the accident and this is often the case. This collision has led to calls for a review of the safety procedures in the Straits, but it is infuriating that it takes a calamitous accident for the authorities to start to look at the problems. Just the dramatic increase in traffic in the region should have started alarm bells ringing.

Collision hot spots

There are quite a few hot spots around the world where ships are forced to pass at close quarters and this must always increase the risk of collision. Narrow and not so narrow channels like the Dover Straits, the Singapore Straits, the Florida Straits, the Bosphorus and the Straits of Messina will always heighten the risk of collision. Approaches to harbours and their entrances also see increased risks, but out in the open sea the possibility of collision still remains. Take the case of the cargo ship that was on passage with the officer on watch doing chart corrections, leaving the seaman lookout watching for other ships. When the lookout went below to carry out fire rounds, the chart correcting continued and the ship collided with a fishing trawler. The fishing boat had seen the ship approaching and had tried to take avoiding action but was hampered by its trawl gear. The resulting damage wasn't serious, but what was unacceptable was firstly, not keeping a lookout, and secondly, carrying on after the collision and not stopping to assist.

Not stopping to assist after a collision is becoming all too common. When a ship collides with a small yacht the crew of the ship may not be aware of the collision taking place, but when two ships collide there should be no mistaking the noise and the bump. When two 4,000 tonne cargo ships collided off Korea, one ship sank very quickly, with the loss of 16 lives. The other ship, although suffering damage at the stern, carried on as though nothing had happened. Were they hoping that if they didn't stop nobody would notice there had been a collision and they would then escape the consequences?

The quality of crews on board ships is acknowledged as deteriorating and this must increase the risk of collision. In one report it was claimed that the new generation of LNG carriers are offering such high rates of pay for qualified officers that they are denuding other ships of experienced operators. Combine this with the fatigue problem that seems to be on the increase among watch keepers and it is not too difficult to see the basic causes of collisions at sea. I have heard ships' officers talk about a lack of trust at sea these days, and in that comment I feel they are referring to not being able to trust those on another ship to take the required action under the Colregs to avoid a collision. You cannot be sure that the other ship has seen or is aware of you until it makes some obvious alteration of course, and by that time things could be getting too close. Those cross-Channel ferry skippers have a point in developing their own system to cope with a situation that appears to have got out of hand. Just assume that everybody else is incompetent and make sure you keep out of their way. When you have 3,000 passengers on board you can't afford to take chances.

Yacht collisions are in the minority

Although there have been a number of high profile reports of collisions between yachts and ships, I am convinced that these are still in the minority compared with ship-ship and ship-fishing vessel collisions. Yachtsmen do not reach the level of fatigue that ships' officers can endure and there should be a lower level of distraction. Yachtsmen usually also have a strong instinct for survival. They have a desire to learn, to expand their knowledge and experience, and this makes them both cautious and careful in any encounters with shipping. There is probably the same of lack of trust that is found among ship's officers, and there is a worrying trend that suggests that in trying to cover every situation, the Colregs have become too complex. They have become more of a legal document, used to decide who is right and who is wrong after a collision has occurred, rather than being a practical set of rules to help the seaman cope with difficult situations at sea.

Ever since that catamaran collision I get very nervous when two boats or ships are running close together. That event made me realise just how small the margins can be when boats are only yards apart. It only takes one small mistake, one failure in the engines or steering, and disaster stares you in the face. There may be times when you have to get close, perhaps to be able to shout across or transfer people but, if necessary, the whole operation should be performed at slow speed. The slower you go, the more time you will have to correct mistakes. Always try to leave a way out in case the unexpected happens.

This is fine when undertaking planned manoeuvres, but at sea there is always the risk of the unexpected and collisions of one sort or another are part of that risk. Probably 70% of these collision risks are avoidable and you have to take potluck with the rest. My record is two collisions in 60 years. Not a frequent occurrence, but they do result in a state of shock that doesn't leave you prepared to cope with the aftermath. After a collision you want to wind the clock back and do the manoeuvre differently, but the disaster has happened and all you can do is to try to pick up the pieces, and certainly stay on scene to help if you can.

MARINE ACCIDENT INVESTIGATION BRANCH

A change of mind

Narrative

What started out as a leisurely passage on the south coast turned into a frightening adventure for the skipper and crew of a motor yacht due to the failure of the master of a high-speed craft (HSC) to appreciate the situation from the yacht's point of view.

On clearing the entrance of the estuary, the master of the HSC retained the con of the vessel and increased speed to about 34 knots. At this time, the chief officer was assisting the master in executing the passage plan.

Visibility was good, and although there was a force 5 wind blowing, the height of the sea was recorded as 0.5m. Both 'X' and 'S' band radars were working, but unfortunately no targets were acquired for plotting and the present traffic was being assessed by eye rather than by all the available means.

The motor yacht was first sighted at about 10 degrees on the starboard bow at a distance of about 3.5nm and appeared to be crossing and on a collision course. The master of the HSC, being the give way vessel, decided to alter course 15 degrees to starboard which, by the time he had done so, put the motor yacht 1.6nm away and fine on his port bow.

For an unexplained reason, the master changed his mind at a distance of about 1nm and altered course to port by about 10 degrees. The astonished skipper of the motor yacht stopped his engines to increase the passing distance, and the HSC passed 2.5 cables ahead. The skipper and crew of the yacht were frightened by the experience, which was made worse by having to brace themselves against the effects of the HSC's wash.

The master of the HSC was unaware that his last minute change of plan had caused so much upset on the yacht. He believed he had the situation under control. The yacht skipper reported the incident to the MAIB and, consequently, the Voyage Data Recorder (VDR) records were retrieved from the HSC. It was only through

analysis of the VDR data that exactly what had occurred could be deduced. Several shortfalls in the bridge team performance were identified and measures were put in place to avoid a similar incident.

The Lessons

1

It is a good idea for ship managers to routinely download the data from the vessel's VDR every now and again to audit the bridge team's performance.

2

Masters and crews on fast merchant vessels, and especially those on HSC, should consider how their planned actions will be seen by smaller, slower craft, yachts and fishing vessels. Although the master was aware of the yacht, and in his mind had the situation totally under control, the yacht skipper had a very different opinion and desperately needed reassurance.

3

Even HSCs must obey the Colregs! In this case, the master of the HSC should have taken early action to clearly indicate his intentions. He should then have maintained his course until past and clear and most definitely should not have changed his mind and altered at the last minute across the bow of the yacht. There was no navigational reason for him to have to pass closer than a mile from any craft in the vicinity.

4

Good bridge teamwork practices require that actions by one person are cross-checked by another member of the team. In this case the chief officer should have questioned the master's intentions/actions.

5

Wash from HSCs can be a serious problem to small craft, even at sea and in deep water. Bridge teams should be sensitive to this fact and plan their actions accordingly.

The future

In researching this book I found it disconcerting that there has not been a significant reduction in the number of disasters that occur at sea. The figures are frighteningly high for an industry that has made a considerable leap into modern technology. Contemporary electronic systems have made navigation easy and relatively reliable, and the structures and strengths of ships and small craft have never been so carefully analysed and calculated. The amount of regulation has increased dramatically and in theory, at least, vessels should be safe. So what has gone wrong if accidents are still occurring so regularly?

There are a number of factors involved, but topping the list is the fact that in my view most technological advances have increased the efficiency of vessels rather than their safety. Forward steps have been matched by a drop in the safety margins used in the operation of shipping and small craft, so that no real advance has been made. The same situation exists on our roads: if an improvement is made in a car's braking system, cars will be driven closer together, cancelling out any progress in safety. Precisely this happened at sea when GPS was introduced as a major advance in navigation accuracy and reliability. It was this reliable accuracy that allowed vessels to reduce their safety margins, because theoretically they knew their exact position and so could pass closer to dangers than before.

Disasters in the modern world

We like to think that the epic marine disasters of the past could not happen in the modern world, but that is not the case. A disaster like the *Titanic* hitting that iceberg (and not having enough lifeboats to evacuate all her passengers and crew) should not be possible with modern technology. However, just recently a passenger ship hit an iceberg and sank. Those on board had to take to open lifeboats. In many ways this was a lucky escape, and could have been so much worse if rescue ships had not been close by. In my opinion safety at sea today still depends very heavily on luck and that does not seem acceptable.

The *Estonia* disaster showed what can happen when luck runs out and bad management takes over. Here was a structural failure that set off a chain of events resulting in a very heavy loss of life. The basic cause can be traced back to human error and the reality is that no amount of technology can compensate for that. We see human error playing an increasing role in accidents at sea these days. As the industry reduces its safety margins in the quest for increased efficiency, any human error can have far-reaching consequences.

Potential collisions

I am convinced that there is a major shipping disaster waiting to happen in the near future. There is a wide choice of possible scenarios. Passenger shipping is at the head of my list, because the large numbers of people involved will make any passenger ship accident headline news. A close second is the rapidly increasing trade in carrying highly flammable liquid gases around the oceans of the world. Each of these potentially lethal floating bombs could devastate the ports and harbours that they operate from. A worst case scenario for the ultimate shipping disaster would involve a full passenger ship in collision with a liquid natural gas carrier.

That may sound like a plot for a disaster movie but it could happen. We need only look at the Dover Straits, one of the busiest shipping channels in the world. Here there are ferries that carry upwards of 2,000 people cutting straight across the path of ships that are carrying these cargoes of liquid gas. If everybody follows the rules then a collision will not occur, but does everybody follow the rules? The evidence suggests they don't. It is recognised that the passenger ferries have set up their own series of rules when operating on these cross-Channel routes in order to increase their level of safety. That is the theory and so far it has been a relatively successful operation. The rules developed by the ferries mean that they operate in lanes. These lanes separate ferries travelling in opposite directions, and they also give way to all other shipping that is travelling in the Straits. It should be stressed that this is what might be called a private system and it seems to have tacit approval from the authorities, but it is not a system that the other ships are aware of and it has no official standing.

The theory is that all the regular shipping travelling up and down the Channel will stay on its regular course and the ferries will take any necessary avoiding action. Because of the busy waters, the distances at which ships pass can be relatively small, in the order of half a mile or less, and for large ships that can be too close for comfort. If everything goes according to plan that margin is fine, but what happens if one ship has a loss of engine power or a steering failure? By the time the problem has been detected by the other ship they could be at very close quarters with a collision imminent. All of the risk analysis in collision avoidance is conducted on radar these days, and it requires considerable skill and fine judgement to make the correct call. In clear weather the visual sighting of the other vessels will help get it right, but these same high-risk operations are also carried out in thick fog. Here the watch officers rely entirely on radar and their own skill and assessment capabilities. No allowances are made in terms of reducing speed because the ferries operate to a very tight schedule.

Accidents waiting to happen

Other areas around the world with dense traffic also give cause for concern. The Straits of Messina between Italy and Sicily, for example, have already seen collisions involving the fast ferries that criss-cross the Straits and there are likely to be more. This shipping passage is so narrow that space for manoeuvring is limited, and it can be difficult to distinguish the lights of ships against the shore lights of the coast. Close-quarters situations are inevitable, and where they exist, collisions will almost invariably follow.

The Straits of Malacca are another area of dense shipping with crossing ferry traffic, much of it at high speed. Not only are the shipping channels relatively narrow but there is a sharp, almost right-angle turn at the western entrance that creates an extra challenge for ships. Much of this traffic comprises large tankers and container ships passing through on their way to Japan and China. Lately ships carrying liquid gas have also joined the crowded shipping lanes. The tidal flow can run at up to 6 knots to add to the challenge. There can often be very heavy rain and even smoke haze to reduce visibility. One report shows 101 collisions in the area over a 16-year period with a further 153 vessels going aground or wrecked. This is a region where accidents are waiting to happen despite traffic separation schemes and other safety measures. With 600 ships a day using the Straits, the odds are stacked against this being an accident-free zone.

In the United States the Florida Straits has similar potential for disaster. With over one million leisure boats around the Florida coast, and 40% of the world's shipping reported to pass through the Straits, the potential is frightening. Some authorities say there are over 1,000 marine accidents each year in this region, but most of those involve leisure craft rather than shipping. Shipping tends to go aground on the valuable coral reefs through navigation mistakes, rather than colliding with other shipping. Yet this is still a cause for great concern as any oil spill here would be devastating.

High on the list of potential disaster areas is the Bosphorus, where shipping numbers and size are increasing. The dangerous twists and turns in this narrow channel are a challenge. When you factor in the high density of ferry traffic that crosses from Europe into Asia across this waterway, and the dense population that lives on the banks of the waterway, there is the potential for a major disaster. The Bosphorus is classed as an international waterway, and as such is open to ships of all nations. Traffic controls have been set up to try to regulate the shipping, but I would put this waterway high on my list of disaster flashpoints.

The problem of tight schedules

The business of keeping to tight schedules is a relatively new feature of shipping. Passenger shipping operates to strict schedules in the interests of providing the sort of reliable service that is demanded by passengers. Increasingly though, we are seeing container shipping operating in a similar manner, having to time their arrival in port to the hour. Any ship operating on a tight time schedule may be tempted to reduce safety margins to cut corners. There are no medals for being late, even if the ship has spent the last 24 hours in thick fog in some of the busiest waters in the world. Picture the scene: a ferry is trying to keep to its timetable in thick fog and is crossing the path of a modern 25 knot, 1,000ft long container ship equally intent on keeping to its schedule. The stakes are high and one day, probably sooner rather than later, somebody is going to get it wrong.

How can such a state of affairs be allowed to continue? How can a non-ice-strengthened passenger ship with 3,000 passengers on board be allowed to operate in ice regions? How can a ship carrying perhaps 100,000 tonnes of liquid gas be allowed to enter a busy port? How can near-miss collision situations be allowed to arise? These are all potentially high-risk shipping scenarios, yet there seems to be no organisation or official body that has the power to stop it in the interests of safety.

Who can stop this happening?

There are people who possess some of this power. A harbour master could stop a ship if he thought it posed a risk to his harbour, but in reality, what harbour master is going to turn ships away? They are operating in a tough commercial environment and if they turn a ship away their competitors are likely to accept it. The people with the power to stop large passenger ships going into the polar regions could be the insurance companies, but again this does not make commercial sense. They may increase premiums to deal with the risk, but that is not much of a deterrent and competitors are always circling looking for business. Classification societies can have some say in what ships can and cannot do, but they are mainly concerned with the structure and the machinery of the ship to ensure that it can operate reasonably safely. They don't have the power to dictate what a ship should or should not do and they must accommodate those owners who want to go bigger and bigger or faster and faster. Ship owners need to find ways forward with new technology and if they don't, their competitors will.

Is it just human error?

As has been emphasised in this book, most accidents at sea are the result of human error; people trying to push the operating envelope or simply not doing what they ought. It tends to be those at the sharp end who get the blame, the navigators on the bridge or the yachtsman at his helm, but so many accidents are caused by technical failures that leave the poor navigator struggling to cope. Most ships and boats have a battery of alarms to warn of a failure, but such alarms sounding in the middle of a critical navigation manoeuvre can divert attention from the job in hand. It is difficult to legislate for such pressures, and there are constant cries for improvements in training and in manning standards. But why should a ship owner spend more money on these things when he is already doing everything that the regulations require? You hear it time and again, when a ship is in trouble or its operations are being questioned: 'We meet all the requirements for safety and operating systems as required by the IMO.' So should the IMO (International Maritime Organisation) play a bigger role in safety at sea?

It was recognised that any agreement about safety at sea would have to be developed by an international body and the IMO was the chosen route. They have made enormous strides in raising the levels of ship safety and operating techniques, but they tend to be reactive rather than proactive. A case in point was the fire on the balconies of a cruise liner. It was only after this fire that rules were hurriedly brought in to ensure that outside balconies were as fireproof as the rest of the ship. I would have thought that any worthwhile risk assessment would have shown up that weakness in fire defences before a fire actually happened.

In my view the IMO tends to tinker around the edges of safety rather than tackling the problems head on. They are generally slow to respond to necessary changes because they must get international agreement and that can be a long, slow process. Some estimates suggest that it can take up to ten years for a change to be brought into effect. National bodies are reluctant to take action on their own because it could mean their ship owners lose the competitive edge. The whole point of IMO was to create a level playing-field for developing safety protocols. Yachting standards are little better, and while designers and builders will meet safety requirements there is no incentive to do anything more.

It is possible to have the best-built and equipped ships in the world but it needs only one small mistake by just one member of the crew for disaster to strike. If only the maritime industry could follow the example of the aircraft industry. Aircraft are built to standard designs tested almost to destruction before being allowed into service, and there are always two people in the cockpit to ensure safety. Frankly, I don't see it happening; we are too entrenched in the current system, so accidents will continue to occur.

Where does this leave us?

Where does this leave yachts and other small craft? Well, most yachts are built to standard designs, which should help to iron out some problems, but I don't know of any builder who tests his boats in any serious way. Usually the prototype has been sold before it is built and the builders work on the premise that the boats will not be used in any seriously adverse conditions. Despite some attempts at directives to improve standards it seems there are few safety features built into production yachts. The industry is thinly regulated and the standards of manning can vary enormously. Yachting seems to have inherited the same casual attitude to safety that is found in shipping, but where yachts may suffer more is when coming into conflict with shipping. A poor standard of lookout and radar equipment means that yachts are practically invisible to ships. They are 'second class citizens' on the water and yacht skippers need to play a defensive game to avoid big ships. In fact, the days of segregation may not be far away.

The marine industry presents a depressing picture. It is a mess, with a distinct lack of control and little incentive to improve. Despite much talk, no one seems to have the power or the resolve to make significant changes to reduce the risk of major disaster. The authorities continue to dabble at the edges of safety improvements, so I forecast disasters at sea will continue and they are likely to become more significant and intense. Major improvements in safety will only be achieved at the expense of the traditional freedom of the sea. If we want to retain that freedom then it is up to seamen and navigators to behave responsibly. Perhaps in 20 years time I will be writing the second edition of this book covering all the most recent disasters at sea. I'm sure there will be plenty of material.

MAIB
MARINE ACCIDENT INVESTIGATION BRANCH

Flooding caused by faulty hull fittings

Narrative

Random Harvest, a 9.86m GRP boat, was returning from an angling trip in the English Channel with eight people on board, including six anglers. Four miles south-west of Brighton the bilge alarm sounded briefly. The skipper lifted the hatch in the wheelhouse and saw the bilges filling with water. He could not identify the source, but started the electric bilge pump and diverted the engine cooling water intake to direct bilge suction. The deckhand operated the manual bilge pump.

The skipper tried to call other vessels in the vicinity, but found the VHF had failed because the batteries had already been covered by floodwater. He used his mobile phone to contact another fishing vessel, *Morning Breeze*, whose skipper relayed the distress to Solent Coastguard. Fortunately, *Random Harvest's* bilge pumping arrangement was able to contain the flooding, and she made her own way towards Brighton, escorted by *Morning Star* and an RNLI lifeboat. Once alongside she was pumped dry and the cause of the leak was discovered: a brass, through-hull, 25mm diameter fitting to the toilet seawater inlet had failed.

In turn, this failure was caused by de-zincification. The fitting had been installed new only 16 months before, so the de-zincification was probably accelerated by stray electrical currents from the vessel's batteries.

Brass is not accepted for use in underwater, through-hull fittings, either by classification societies or by the MCA because of its susceptibility to de-zincification.

During the course of the investigation it was found that some suppliers were unwittingly selling brass fittings incorrectly labelled as bronze. This was brought to their attention.

The Lessons

1

Always ensure that through-hull fittings and seacocks are of an approved material such as silicon bronze, gunmetal or de-zincification resistant (DZR) brass. Be wary of purchasing fittings made from a material that is described by a trade name and not a recognisable metal alloy, and ask for details of its constituent metals. Rather than lose your boat, and possibly lives, it is better to pay a few pounds more for an approved fitting.

2

Reduce the likelihood of stray electrical currents and the possibility of rapid electrolytic corrosion of underwater metal fittings by following good electrical installation practice such as isolating the positive pole of the battery when the vessel is left at her moorings.

3

The battery supplying electricity to the VHF radio and other emergency equipment should be placed in a position where it is less likely to be affected by flooding.

4

The bilge alarm gave early warning, and alerted those on board to the flooding. The outcome might have been very different had the flooding continued undetected – especially as the VHF was disabled before it was discovered.

5

Although the use of mobile telephones as a means of alerting others to incidents and emergencies at sea creates genuine difficulties, it is an invaluable tool when all else fails.

MARINE ACCIDENT INVESTIGATION BRANCH

Marine Accident Investigation Branch

The Marine Accident Investigation Branch (MAIB) is an independent part of the Department for Transport. The Chief Inspector of Marine Accidents is responsible to the Secretary of State for Transport.

Extract from The Merchant Shipping (Accident Reporting and Investigation) Regulations 1999

The fundamental purpose of investigating an accident under these Regulations is to determine its circumstances and the cause with the aim of improving the safety of life at sea and the avoidance of accidents in the future. It is not the purpose to apportion liability, nor, except so far as is necessary to achieve the fundamental purpose, to apportion blame.

Leisure craft accident reports have appeared regularly in the MAIB Safety Digest over the past eight years. As with all MAIB reports, the objective has been to describe the basic facts, and to highlight the lessons to be learned. The Digest, of which three issues are produced each year, is distributed widely in printed form and is also available online at: www.maib.gov.uk.

Much of the MAIB's work is involved with investigating accidents to merchant ships and fishing vessels, and these appear in their own sections in each Safety Digest. The third section in each issue contains, typically, three or four reports relating to leisure craft, sail and power.

The MAIB have published a compendium *Leisure Craft Safety Digest*. This compendium contains 25 of these articles in one easy-to-refer-to volume. It has been produced in response to many requests from sailing schools and establishments, Yachtmaster instructors, and individual sailors and power-boat owners. I very much hope that it will become an important resource for all those who take to the water in small boats, enabling more people to learn important safety lessons.

Stephen Meyer
Chief Inspector of Marine Accidents

If you wish to report an accident or incident please call the MAIB 24 hour reporting line on 023 8023 2527.

The telephone number for general use is 023 8039 5500.

The Branch fax number is 023 8023 2459.

The email address is maib@dft.gsi.gov.uk

Safety Digests are also available on the Internet: www.maib.gov.uk

Index

Acknowledgements

We are grateful to the Marine Accident Investigation Branch for permission to publish the reports at the end of chapters throughout this book.

They provide actual examples of what can go wrong if insufficient care is taken in the potentially dangerous marine environment.

Whatever type of boat the example cites, advice and warnings can be equally applied to any vessel of any size or type.